WORKBOOK FOR
OPENING INNOVATION

Bridging Networked Business,
Intellectual Property and Contracting

Series on Technology Management*

Series Editor: J. Tidd (University of Sussex, UK)   ISSN 0219-9823

*The complete list of the published volumes in the series can be found at
http://www.worldscientific.com/series/stm

SERIES ON TECHNOLOGY MANAGEMENT – VOL. 21

WORKBOOK FOR OPENING INNOVATION

Bridging Networked Business, Intellectual Property and Contracting

Jaakko Paasi
Katri Valkokari
Henri Hytönen
VTT Technical Research Centre of Finland, Finland

Laura Huhtilainen
Soili Nystén-Haarala
University of Eastern Finland, Finland

Imperial College Press

ICP

Published by

Imperial College Press
57 Shelton Street
Covent Garden
London WC2H 9HE

Distributed by

World Scientific Publishing Co. Pte. Ltd.
5 Toh Tuck Link, Singapore 596224
USA office: 27 Warren Street, Suite 401-402, Hackensack, NJ 07601
UK office: 57 Shelton Street, Covent Garden, London WC2H 9HE

British Library Cataloguing-in-Publication Data
A catalogue record for this book is available from the British Library.

Series on Technology Management — Vol. 21
WORKBOOK FOR OPENING INNOVATION
Bridging Networked Business, Intellectual Property and Contracting

Copyright © 2013 by Imperial College Press

ISBN 978-1-84816-960-9

Typeset by Stallion Press
Email: enquiries@stallionpress.com

Printed in Singapore.

Preface

Open and networked innovation is a tenet of business research and practice. It is true that the opening of innovation will create lots of opportunities for new business for a firm. Extant literature of open innovation, however, mainly focuses on underlining the opportunities related to the opening of innovation either by reporting success stories or analysing the phenomenon from an academic viewpoint. Little is written to give practical guidance for managers to support successful implementation of open and networked innovation in business. In the literature of business network management, there are practical tools available for network management, but they are mostly addressing the efficiency and control of the network — not innovation. The guidance given in the literature for making intellectual property (IP) strategy typically focuses on intra-firm aspects only, neglecting inter-firm innovation and open source communities as well as business development in relationships with them. Also, extant literature for business contracting gives little practical support for open and networked innovation.

The *Workbook for Opening Innovation — Bridging Networked Business, Intellectual Property and Contracting* attempts to fill the hole in innovation and business management literature related to the implementation of open and networked innovation in business. The workbook focuses on the implementation of phenomena, theories, and ideas presented in another book by the same authors: *Bazaar of Opportunities for New Business Development — Bridging Networked Innovation, Intellectual Property and Business*. In this book we went beyond the paradigm of open innovation and underlined the variety of opportunities that firms may have in the innovation and new business development with external actors (the term new business development covers here actions for both new business and the renewal of existing business). External actors, however, mean additional risks for the firm that they should manage. In the *Workbook for Opening Innovation* we give practical tools for managers in order for them to be better prepared for innovation with external actors and, accordingly, successfully implement open and networked innovation in their business. Although the workbook is connected with the book *Bazaar of Opportunities*, the former can be used without the latter if one is not interested in arguments and research behind the guides, tools, and check-lists given in the workbook.

The workbook is a result of the multidisciplinary research project "Intellectual Property in Open Business Models" (IPOB), the main project partners of which were VTT Technical Research Centre of Finland and University of Eastern Finland. The multidisciplinary project team consisted of experts in innovation management, business network management, project management, business contracting, IP law, and IP valuation. In parallel with the research project, there was an industry driven project, IPOB Industry, where the research results of IPOB Research were directly applied to the business development cases of the firms of IPOB Industry: Arcusys, Blancco, Medisize, Outotec, Sandvik, and Tamlink. So the guides, tools, and check-lists presented in the workbook have been field tested and improved in the above mentioned firms in real business cases.

The *Workbook for Opening Innovation* is aimed at business managers, research and development (R&D) managers, innovation managers, IP managers, legal counsels, contract designers, project managers, etc., who are involved in networked innovation and business development in one way or another. The target of the book is to bridge and align networked business, IP management, and contracting aspects of a firm to support the business goals of the firm through the opening of innovation. Therefore, experts would be encouraged to read all parts of the workbook in order to have the bridged and aligned standpoint of practices related to the implementation of open and networked innovation in their business (although the experts may find those parts of the book that are close to their special field of expertise relatively basic). We believe that the strength of the book is in the presentation of business, IP management, and contract design standpoints in a coherent manner under the same cover, and in this way to promote the mutual understanding and interaction of business managers, engineers, lawyers, etc., in firms, which is one prerequisite of the successful opening of innovation in firms.

The authors thank Tuija Rantala at VTT, Nari Lee at Hanken School of Economics, Helsinki, and Marko Torkkeli at Lappeenranta University of Technology for useful discussions related to the scientific part of the study; Jari Erkkilä, Vesa Nisula, and Johanna Hakulinen at Tamlink Oy; Jussi Hurskainen at Arcusys Oy, Sergey Vasiliev, Kim Väisänen and Mikko Koponen at Blancco Oy; Juha Laiho and Marita Salo at Medisize Oy; Marja Lahonen and Markku Uoti at Outotec Oyj; Kristina Kirveskoski, Veikko Räisänen, Erkki Ahola, Riku Pulli, and Marko Jokinen at Sandvik Mining and Construction Oy for useful discussions, comments and feedback related to the guides, tools, and check-lists presented in the book; Sisko Mäensivu at VTT for the finalizing of figures; and the Finnish Funding Agency for Technology and Innovation — Tekes for supporting the project in part.

Jaakko Paasi
Katri Valkokari
Henri Hytönen
Laura Huhtilainen
Soili Nystén-Haarala

Tampere, 19 January 2012

About the Authors

Jaakko Paasi

Dr. Jaakko Paasi is a Principal Scientist at VTT Technical Research Centre of Finland. His doctoral thesis (in 1995) was in the field of electrical physics. Gradually his career moved towards studying business and technology management, with a special focus on innovation management. He has written about 100 reviewed scientific articles on magnet technology, superconductivity, electrostatics and innovation management.

Katri Valkokari

PhD Katri Valkokari is a Senior Scientist and team leader at VTT Technical Research Centre of Finland. Her research over past ten years has focused on management and development of business networks. In 2009 Katri Valkokari concluded her doctoral thesis on business network development. She has published several international and national articles in the research areas of strategic business networks, collaboration, organizational knowledge, and innovation management.

Henri Hytönen

Henri Hytönen, Lic.Sc. (Tech.), M.Sc. (Tech), is a Doctoral Student at Aalto University School of Science. His research interests include IPR valuation and management, investment appraisal, and real option valuation methods. The research for the book was done while he was a Research Scientist at VTT Technical Research Centre of Finland.

Laura Huhtilainen

Laura Huhtilainen is a Doctoral Student at the University of Eastern Finland. Her research interests are related to contracting in the context of networked innovation and business.

Soili Nystén-Haarala

Soili Nystén-Haarala, LL.D., M.Sc. (Econ.), is Professor of Civil Law at the University of Eastern Finland. In her doctoral dissertation she compared the logics of contract law applied by courts with logics of business. Since then she has written on proactive law and contracting as well as on developing Russian law in its social, economic and political circumstances. She has led several research projects on these themes. From July 2011 she has also worked as a part-time professor of law at Luleå University of Technology in Sweden.

Contents

Part I

INTRODUCTION

Chapter 1

Introduction

The importance of innovations as a source of economic growth, competitiveness, and wellbeing is almost universally recognized today. Innovations and the consequent renewal of business are the key to the long-term success of firms. Firms that do not innovate will die sooner or later.

There are various definitions given in the literature for the term "innovation". In this book we use the definition which states that innovation is a new idea that can be commercialized and is significantly better than an earlier solution (Paasi *et al.*, 2012). The innovation can relate to products, services, technologies, business and organizational models, operational processes, or operational methods. This definition of innovation underlines the connection to business development and commercialization of innovation, i.e. innovation initiatives should be clearly connected to business and intellectual property (IP) strategies of actors.

Innovative endeavours of firms nowadays commonly take place in interaction between two or more organizations. Single firms as organizational systems alone do not emerge with innovation, except in a minority of cases. Designs of new innovation, however, are often developed internally by individual companies that keep strategic control over their designs (DeBresson, 1999; Laursen and Salter, 2006; Maxwell, 2006).

Openness in innovation is not a new practice. Several authors have argued that a fully closed innovation approach is an exception in history (DeBresson, 1999; Maxwell, 2006; Mowery, 2009). In the past, the innovation interaction, however, was restricted to face-to-face meetings, mainly in the neighbourhood. In the 1990s, openness started to emerge as a major global phenomenon due to changes in the social, technological, and competitive environment. Its emergence can be tied to technological developments such as digitization and the growth of the internet, the increased complexity of products, the shortening of technology life cycles, the growing importance of services, the emergence of new markets, globalization, and dispersed value chains. These all forced firms to search new forms of external co-operation and open their new innovation and business development processes (see e.g. Chesbrough, 2003; Chiaramonte, 2006; Henkel, 2006; Maxwell, 2006; West and Gallagher, 2006; Dittrich and Duysters, 2007; IfM and IBM, 2007; van der Vrande *et al.*, 2009).

The increased openness and inter-firm collaboration in innovation with various different forms led business researchers to develop theories and models to describe the emerging phenomena. Perhaps the most famous one is the paradigm of "Open Innovation" by Henry Chesbrough (2003). Chesbrough assigned a single term (open innovation) to a collection of developments that enabled both academics and practitioners to rethink innovation strategies in a networked world.

According to Chesbrough (2006a, p. 1): "Open Innovation processes combine internal and external ideas into architectures and systems. They utilize business models to define the requirements for these architectures and systems. The business model utilizes both external and internal ideas to create value, while defining internal mechanisms to claim some portion of that value." Another term often used in connection with open innovation is "Open Business Models" which underlines the importance of business models when acting in the landscape of open innovation, as described above.

Chesbrough's concept of open innovation is (probably intentionally) very loosely defined. The loose definition encourages people to find new ways to explore and exploit innovations more or less openly in a networked world but, at the same time, may make the actual open innovation actions challenging as the coherent understanding of open innovation practices between actors may be deficient (Luoma *et al.*, 2010; Huizingh, 2011). That is particularly true for the openness in open innovation, which simply cannot be considered as a dichotomy, such as open versus closed or public versus proprietary.

In the book *Bazaar of Opportunities for New Business Development – Bridging Networked Innovation, Intellectual Property and Business* (Paasi *et al.*, 2012) we discussed the opening of innovation for external actors.

Involvement of external actors may open up lots of new opportunities for a firm to create new business or to renew an existing business: the firm can utilize external knowledge or technology to create new offerings, and the firm can find external paths to commercialize its knowledge or technology. We compared today's networked business environment to oriental bazaars, and to the being and dealing in the bazaar with known and unknown actors, in order to better visualize strategies and actions related to open and networked innovation in business networks.

In this *Workbook for Opening Innovation* we will focus on the implementation of ideas and theories presented in the Bazaar of Opportunities into the practice. We will present guides, tools, and check-lists that will support firms in gaining from open and networked innovation. The workbook is divided into four parts that focus on opening innovation from different standpoints:

- Part I: Introduction
- Part II: Networked Business
- Part III: IP Strategy
- Part IV: Practices and Actions

Part I is an introduction to the actual workbook parts of the book (Parts II–IV). In Part I we will give a frame for opening innovation in networked business. The actual guides, tools, and check-lists will be given in Parts II–IV. Part II "Networked Business" and Part III "IP Strategy" are aimed at supporting management and decision making at strategic and tactical levels of business. Part IV "Practices and Actions" is aimed to give support for daily actions at an operational level. The parts and their elements are not independent from each other but form a triangle of opening innovation in networked business (Fig. 1.1).

The elements of Part II "Networked Business" consist of a description of the variety of used collaboration models in networked innovation and business (Chapter 4), and a guide for collaboration in networked business (Chapter 5). The elements of Part III "IP Strategy" include a description of IP strategy in the context of open and networked innovation (Chapter 6), and a guide for making such an IP strategy (Chapter 7). Finally, the elements of Part IV "Practices and Actions" give a range of tools including a description of methods available for knowledge protection in networked

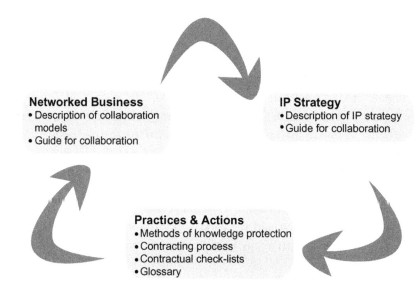

Fig. 1.1.   Elements of the opening of innovation in networked business.

business (Chapter 8), guidance for contracting (Chapter 9), practical check-lists supporting contractual issues of open and networked innovation and business (Chapter 10), and a glossary (Chapter 11).

The use of the tools presented in this workbook is illustrated through case examples by using a fictitious story and fictitious firms. The fictitious story and firms will be presented in Chapter 5.

The arguments for why this workbook contains, particularly, the parts and elements shown in Fig. 1.1 are given in the book *Bazaar of Opportunities for New Business Development*. Here in the *Workbook for Opening Innovation* we just summarize that, to be successful at opening innovation in networked business, an actor must understand its own role and interests as well as those of the opponents, know the value of the offering in question, be creative and skilful in negotiating and agreeing, understand the business model in question and what opportunities and limitations that will create, etc. In an innovation network involving multiple actors and sources of innovation there should be openness and trust otherwise the innovation network will not be successful in the long-term. It is a great challenge to build up and maintain a network that can systemically create new innovations. Questions related to IP are an important part of the challenge. The wrong kind of focus and policy on IP would easily kill open ideation and conceptualization in the network. On the other hand, the right kind of focus and policy on IP can stimulate systemic generation of new innovations in the innovation network. The practical innovation and new business development work should also be aligned with contracting and contracts. In open and networked innovation, contracts should not be seen just as safeguarding documents of networked business. Instead, contracting and contracts are tools for the co-ordination of innovation and new business development actions. Trust between the actors of innovation will be strengthened and brought from personal to organizational level by contracts.

Before going on to Chapters 2–11, we would like to discuss knowledge and the term intellectual property (IP). Intellectual property and IP strategy are important issues of new business development both in closed and open innovation models. The legal institution of intellectual property is based on the metaphor of static and linear understanding of the innovation process. Accordingly, it stimulates stand-alone innovation by single firms. This is in contrast with the fluid, flexible and complex operational (business) process of a firm that has opened its innovation work to external actors in order to create new business.

In the practice of law, IP may include rights on, among others, patent, copyright, trademark, trade secrecy, rights in the topography of integrated circuits, industrial design rights, plant breeders' rights, publicity rights, and database rights. In terms of knowledge, IP law may include rights related to explicit, codified knowledge. However, explicit knowledge plays only one part of a firm's knowledge resources. There is also a tacit part of knowledge (often called know-how) that often makes a difference in a firm's performance. Legal protection of the tacit part of knowledge, however, is unclear. Only explicit, codified knowledge can have clear legal protection (Teece, 1998). According to the interview study of the IPOB project (Paasi *et al.*, 2010), firms would like to isolate and control the tacit knowledge related to inter-organizational innovation. Attempts to do that include contracts, company policies, and the use of the term "intellectual property" in contracts in a broad sense.

The practice of firms to use the term IP in a broad sense, which may further differ from firm to firm, may cause misunderstandings and consequent problems in networked innovation. Thus it is crucial to align the practice of the firms and, to do so, all parties need to have one coherent understanding of the term. The interest of firms in also isolating and controlling the know-how related to networked innovation is well understood and justified. Therefore,

> *In this workbook we will use the term "intellectual property" broadly to include not only IP rights that are granted and protected by laws, but also the knowledge and other intangible resources, whose use may be controlled by contracts, policies, organization, and process routines and norms, both physically and technically.*

The definition is the same as that which we used in the book *Bazaar of Opportunities for New Business Development – Bridging Networked Innovation, Intellectual Property and Business.*

Chapter 2

Opening Innovation

Successful implementation of guides, tools, and check-lists to be presented in Parts II–IV of this workbook calls for some basic and coherent understanding of the opening of innovation. Therefore, we complete the introductory part of the book with a somewhat theoretical discussion about openness in innovation, derive a framework for opening innovation with different characteristic levels of openness, and give examples for the characteristic levels of openness in innovation.

In the literature of open innovation, openness has a variety of different meanings. Firstly, the openness in open innovation may refer to a variety of inbound and outbound innovation activities and forms, including acquiring, sourcing, selling, and revealing of IP (Gassmann and Enkel, 2004; Dahlander and Gann, 2010). Secondly, it may also refer to the number of external sources of innovation (Laursen and Salter, 2006), or, thirdly, to the flow of knowledge, including the aspects of knowledge exploration, retention, and exploitation (Lichtenthaler and Lichtenthaler, 2009). Fourthly, openness may be related to the innovation process and to the innovation outcome which could be closed (proprietary) or open (available to others) (Chesbrough, 2003; Maxwell, 2006; Huizingh, 2011). Based on the openness of both the process and the outcome of innovation, Huizingh (2011) developed a 2×2 matrix depending on whether the process and its outcome are closed or open (i.e. available to others). Fifthly, openness can be related to the actors of open innovation, whether they are known or not (Paasi *et al.*, 2011). In bilateral works and in closed consortia actors know each other but public societies, open communities, and forums contain unknown actors of open innovation. The five items listed above are not independent. Instead they are more or less related to each other. They consider the same phenomenon but they approach the phenomenon from partially different standpoints.

In this workbook we follow the line of Chesbrough (2003), Maxwell (2006), and Huizingh (2011) and consider the actual open innovation work, because the various inbound and outbound forms and activities of open innovation as well as the internal and external knowledge flow can be taken into account when studying the actual innovation work. In order to do that, however, we must consider in addition to the innovation process and the innovation outcome the input to the innovation process as well (Paasi *et al.*, 2011). We define characteristic levels of openness in innovation (process) with the aim of creating a framework that would help firms in defining an appropriate form of collaboration, managing knowledge sharing and IP during and after the collaboration, writing contract clauses to formalize the collaboration, etc.

Related to the innovation outcome, Maxwell (2006) found that innovation works could be characterized in (at least) three different ways according to availability, accessibility, and responsibility of the innovation outcome. Within the context of open innovation, we define availability as openness of input knowledge (both explicit and tacit) inside the network of actors. The input is evaluated and analysed in order to gather know-how, background information, and IP relevant to the subject of collaboration. Accordingly, availability as a level of openness refers to works where the input is open but the process and its output are closed. The second characteristic term of Maxwell, accessibility, refers to openness of both the input and the process, e.g. agreement about co-development of knowledge between the known actors of open innovation. The third of Maxwell's characteristic terms, work's responsiveness, defines the potential for modifying it based on contributions from others. In our framework the broad responsiveness corresponds to modifiability which refers to a more transparent co-creation process where the actors can take part in each other's development work. Thereby, we have defined three levels of openness in open innovation. A fourth level, located at the closed end of the levels, is the closed model of open innovation which refers to an internal innovation process of a firm where external knowledge or IP is bought (or internal knowledge or IP is sold) through a transaction within a frame of bilateral contract or a one-way open knowledge acquisition process. The latter includes the collection of customer and end-user information for an input of innovation without co-creational mutual conversation during the collection process.

A fifth level of openness can be defined as the open end of the levels when we follow the line of Paasi *et al.* (2011) and distinguish whether the innovation work is public (i.e. available, accessible, and modifiable by all) or open only within a closed consortium (i.e. available, accessible, and modifiable only among the partners of the consortium under an agreement). Accordingly, we define public as the fifth level of openness. The public refers to the most open models of innovation where both the input and output are open, modifiable, and exploitable to all participants. The open participation means that the process may include unknown actors.

The five levels of openness in innovation form a framework for opening innovation (see Table 2.1). The framework is based on a systematic and nearly mathematical approach towards the openness. Still it has its roots in the extant literature of open innovation. It considers openness in the input for innovation, in the actual innovation process, and in the innovation outcome. Secondly, it considers openness with respect to actors: is the innovation work only open for a restricted number of known actors or is it also open for unknown actors?

From a mathematical viewpoint, four different levels could be distinguished for the open innovation within both closed and open relationships, but in practice that four-level categorization may make sense only for open

Table 2.1.   Five levels of openness in innovation — the framework for opening innovation.

Name of level	Closed	Available	Usable	Modifiable	Public
Key characteristic of openness	IP transaction only	Open innovation within closed bi- or multilateral (network) relationships			Open innovation within open networks
Input for innovation	closed (transaction)	open	open	open	open
Innovation process	closed	closed	open	open	open
Innovation outcome	closed	closed	closed	open	open

innovation within closed relationships and networks with known actors. In open networks, openness with respect to innovation input, process, and outcome means the same as public. In the "closed" openness level, public knowledge and IP can be used as an input for the innovation work but, as the transaction of knowledge or IP is unilateral, the situation is essentially the same as in the case of a transaction under a closed relationship. Innovation in the restricted levels of openness, namely in the levels "available" and "usable", calls for discussions between the actors, and discussions with restricted openness can be done only with known actors (the actors can be previously unknown but they become known during the work). "Modifiable" is the level of full openness but, in order to make a difference between situations where the openness applies only within a closed relationship or consortium and where the work is public (i.e. modifiable by all), there should be a separate level of openness for fully open innovation works with open access. Thus, we conclude with the five distinct levels of openness in Table 2.1.

How are these five levels of openness realized in the practices of open and networked innovation? What are the main characteristics of the levels? Below we will review the five levels, level by level, and try to answer the above questions.

The openness level "closed" is perhaps the most common form of open innovation where two actors are involved in the innovation work. The name "closed" comes from the way the actors open up the actual innovation work with each other. In the level "closed", they tend to share their knowledge with the other actors as little as possible during the actual development work. The interaction between the actors is based on the contractual transaction of IP (IP understood in the broad sense as discussed in Chapter 1) that is used as an input for the actual (closed) development work. The transacted IP may include not only formal IP rights, but also other kinds of explicit knowledge that could be transacted from one actor to another. The former type of transacted IP includes buying and selling of patents and other formal IP as well as licensing of patents. The latter consists of sourced (subcontracted) expertise work with minimal interaction between the principal and the agent and opening of knowledge from the principal to the agent.

Nowadays there are lots of firms that are searching for external technologies which could be integrated into their own products and services.

There are firms that are searching for external technologies which they could build into a winning business model and then commercialize the technology. There are also technology developers who are searching for partners for the commercialization of their technology. Firms are also searching for special expertise knowledge to be used as input for the closed innovation development work inside the company. And there are firms that are offering those kinds of research, technology, and innovation services. When the innovation work between the provider of services and the principal takes place with minimal opening of tacit knowledge to each other during the work, we can speak about IP transaction only and the work belongs to the openness category of "closed". But when the innovation work is accompanied with essential opening of tacit knowledge during the process, we speak about an openness level of "usable" or "modifiable" (see below).

The openness level "available" is related to open innovation where the actors of closed bi- or multilateral relationship contractually share a common input material for the innovation work but then complete the work independently. The level "available" has much in common with the level "closed". In both levels the actual innovation process is more or less closed and the openness is restricted to the input for innovation. But there are two major differences between the levels "available" and "closed". Firstly, in the level "available" there can be more than two actors involved either through bi- or multilateral (consortium) contracts of collaboration. Secondly, the input does not have to be based on a transaction of IP from one party to another but sharing of input knowledge with other parties in collaboration; changes to the ownership structures of the input IP are not required. An example of practical innovation work under the category of "available" is a contractual establishment of a common knowledge platform above which the partners of the consortium could independently develop and commercialize their own applications. That is, the parties agree about strategic collaboration in order to build a common knowledge base in order to support proprietary development and commercialization of their own IP using the common knowledge base. The common knowledge base could be created either by sharing (making readable) their own existing knowledge of the principal actors or by jointly sourcing the input from a third party.

The openness level "usable" covers a broad range of open innovation activities having similar levels of openness. The level "usable" is a typical way of doing innovation projects where two or more actors open and share their knowledge with each other and by this way co-create something new. The work takes place in a closed relationship or consortium and is defined by an agreement. The actors can freely utilize the input (background) material during the development work (project). They agree in the (consortium) agreement what the conditions are under which they can use the input after the work. The actual innovation process is characterized by co-development between some or all members of the network. All members have the right to observe each other's development work. Ownership and utilization of the innovation outcome (IP) is also agreed between the network members. A commonly used principle is where the inventor owns the IP and the other parties have a right to utilize (license) it under agreed conditions. It may also be that the IP will be owned by an actor who has the best potential to commercialize it successfully. Although the process will end up as proprietary (closed) IP, it does not necessarily mean that the owner of the IP will have all the future profits due to the IP. The actors of co-creation may agree on how the future profits will be shared. To operate successfully under the "usable" category of open and networked innovation, there must be a good fit between the roles and business interests of the actors across the consortium. It is also important that questions related to the innovation input, process, and outcomes are agreed between all the actors in appropriate depth.

Research and development projects supported by the European Commission or by a national public funding agency typically have an openness that can be characterized by the term "usable". Naturally, there are lots of exceptions to that, but a typical public-funded consortium project is characterized by: co-development between some or all members of the network; all members having the right to observe each other's development work; and the results of the work are not joint, and instead the network members come to an agreement about the ownership and utilization of the IP. The level "usable", however, is not restricted to R&D projects with public funding. There are lots of privately funded, inter-firm business projects that are characterized by more or less open sharing of knowledge during the innovation work, co-creation with some or all members of the networks, but that end up as proprietary (closed) IP in accordance with the project (business) agreement.

The openness level "modifiable" is the most open form of innovation that takes place within closed relationships with known actors. In this level we can speak about truly open innovation with known actors, where the input for innovation, the actual innovation process, and the innovation outcome are open, but open only for the members of the closed consortium. The level "modifiable" differs from the level "usable" in two senses. Firstly, the innovation leads to joint IP (joint ownership and utilization). The joint ownership, however, may not necessarily mean joint patenting. Instead, it may mean a contractual arrangement where the structures of IP ownership and rights to utilize the IP are contractually arranged in a way in which the members of the network will have equal rights to utilize, modify, and build business above the jointly developed IP. Secondly, the openness related to the input and the process is more controlled in the level "usable" than at the level "modifiable". At the level "modifiable", the input (background material) is freely modifiable by the actors, the actors take part in each other's development work, which means sharing of tacit knowledge with each other, and the results of co-development work are shared between the actors. Basically, the principles are very similar to those of open source societies, with the exception that the participation in the work is not open.

There is a wide range of innovation work that fits under the category "modifiable", from bilateral innovation relationships to large consortia with 20–30 partners. Some of the works are pre-commercial in their nature meaning that the innovation is explorative leading to results that cannot be directly commercialized. Such joint works may result in a common knowledge base which the members of the network can later on develop and independently own products and services to be commercialized. Pre-commerciality, however, is not a characteristic feature in the level "modifiable". There are also innovation works whose results can directly be successfully commercialized. Such works can be bilateral co-creation projects that take place at the interface of firms' knowledge base or open source kind of projects where the participation is limited to known actors defined at the beginning of the work. The main motivation for running open source-type projects within a closed consortium is the control that the actors have over the knowledge that they share with the consortium, as the other actors will be known to them. Thus they can be sure that their competitors are not directly or indirectly involved in the work, which makes a big difference to what they can and will share with the other members of the innovation network. Managers who have lots of experience on innovation works under the level "modifiable" have said that these kind of open innovation projects are challenging because, in order to be successful, the actors must really share the view on the objectives of collaboration and on the degree of openness required to reach the objectives before, during, and after the project (Paasi *et al.*, 2011).

The openness level "public" is the ultimate form of open innovation. At this level, not only are the input, the process, and the outcome open, but the whole work is available, accessible, and modifiable to everyone, i.e. it is public. The fact that it is public and open for all, however, does not mean that there are no limiting conditions for the accessibility and modifiability of the work. Typically there are well-specified rules for the accessibility and modifiability of the work. Open source projects are a good example of that. In open source projects the participation is open but controlled and, in order to utilize the results, one must accept the licence conditions of the project. Open source software projects are the most common (but not the only) examples of "public" open innovation projects.

The discussion above is summarized in Table 2.2. This table gives a framework for the design and management of practical innovation projects. The systematic categorization of openness levels will help project managers, contract and IP management designers to gain a shared view of openness in a particular innovation project, and, thereby, to define an appropriate form of collaboration, to manage knowledge sharing and IP during and after the collaboration, and to write contract clauses to formalize the collaboration. The shared view will also help project co-ordinators in the development of a convincing development agenda and to communicate it clearly to each partner in the innovation work, thus supporting the actual innovation work. All this will be discussed in more detail in Parts II–IV of the workbook.

The frameworks in Tables 2.1 and 2.2 are based on the consideration of openness related to the input, process, and outcome of innovation. As described in the beginning of the chapter, however, there are also other ways to consider the opening of innovation. Therefore, in some contexts it might be more appropriate to consider transparency of innovation work instead of openness (the bottom row in Table 2.2). At the "closed" end of the openness, the innovation process is non-transparent; neither the input

Table 2.2. Main characteristics of the levels of openness in innovation.

Name of level	Closed	Available	Usable	Modifiable	Public
Key characteristics	IP transaction within closed, bilateral agreements	Collaborative models of innovation within bilateral or multilateral relationships			Public innovation processes within open networks
Input for innovation	Own R&D and sourced knowledge	Shared (readable) during the development work	Freely utilized within the consortium partners during the development work	Input is the object of co-development and freely modifiable by consortium members	Public (open and modifiable and exploitable to all)
Innovation process	Closed development	Closed own development, opened to network members based on own decision	Co-development between some or all members, network members have right to observe each other's development work	Results of co-development work will be shared, network members take part to each other's development work	Participation open but typically controlled (might include unknown actors)
Innovation outcome	Proprietary own IP and confidentiality	Proprietary own IP	Ownership and utilization of IP agreed between the network members	Joint IP (ownership and rights to utilize)	Public
Transparency	Non-transparent	Translucent	Translucent	Translucent	Transparent

nor output knowledge is shared between the actors, but they can be a target of business transaction. "Available", "usable", and "modifiable" are all translucent levels of innovation. At the availability level, the input is transparent, while the innovation process and output are non-transparent. The openness at the "available" level means making an innovation process to welcome input knowledge from a wide set of innovation makers. At the "usable" level the input knowledge is transparent, the innovation process is translucent, but the output knowledge is non-transparent. The openness in the "usable" level stands for making input and process accessible to others. At the "modifiable" level the input knowledge, the innovation process, and the output are transparent to the involved network actors. The openness at the level "modifiable" is all about making an innovation process capable of debating distinct points of views and making the decisions related to the process transparent to involved actors. When transparency is present, flow of knowledge must be reciprocal, e.g. both outside-in and inside-out innovation actions exist between the network actors. At the public end the innovation process is transparent; both the input and the output knowledge is shared between the actors. The openness at the "public" level signifies the making of the innovation process available to other actors, who may even be unknown, as well as making the outcomes accessible to others as well. This kind of openness increases the range of ideas and viewpoints, thereby promoting innovation and the development of new solutions.

Part II

NETWORKED BUSINESS

Networked Business
- Description of collaboration models
- Guide for collaboration

IP Strategy
- Description of IP strategy
- Guide for collaboration

Practices & Actions
- Methods of knowledge protection
- Contracting process
- Contractual check-lists
- Glossary

Chapter 3

Networked Business Environment

When open innovation processes cross over the boundaries of a firm towards the networked business environment, there are several models of inter-organizational, networked innovation initiatives. The levels of openness presented in Chapter 2 described different practices of inter-organizational co-operation and collaboration within it. Figure 3.1 illustrates different co-operation surfaces of a networked business environment: a firm's internal co-operation, value networks, intentional collaboration within networked business environment, and macro-level networks.

In the present network economy firms are already used to co-operating with their suppliers and customers, i.e. the members of their value network who are involved in the production of the current products of a firm. These relationships can even be defined by the firm's business strategy and business model. Thus, the other surfaces, networked business environment, and macro-level industrial networks are typically not so well understood or considered within the strategic decisions of firms. In this workbook we distinguish intentional collaboration from loosely coupled macro-level industrial networks by the concept of networked innovation.

Intentional collaboration is generally understood as a mutually beneficial and well-defined relationship entered into by two or more organizations to achieve results they are more likely to achieve together than alone (Möller *et al.*, 2005). In the context of networked business, intentional collaboration is a means to carry through strategic targets and improve the future competitiveness of collaboration partners. This kind of intentional collaboration, for instance different models of strategic networks, partnerships, and alliances, has several — partly overlapping — definitions in

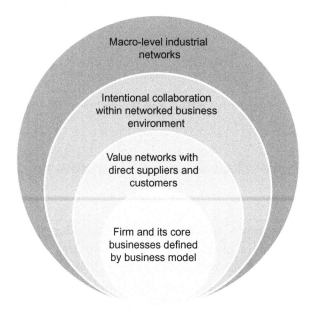

Fig. 3.1.   Different levels in the networked business environment.

the management literature. In proportion, there are numerous collaboration models in company practices.

In the next chapter we will gather the different collaboration models that will be further discussed in the subsequent chapters. These collaboration models, as well as companies' business development needs in general, can be distinguished by their targets. The target of collaboration can be either: (1) exploitation of current knowledge, or (2) exploration of new knowledge and business opportunities. In networked innovation and business, a strategic approach is required at both the overall collaboration level and in network member firms, in order to fuel growth and strengthen the future competitiveness of a firm.

As a model of organizing, these different collaboration models settle between open markets and closed hierarchies, e.g. firms. Thus, their co-ordination is based both on formal control-governance and informal self-organization through social interactions between network actors. Collaboration is an intentional and interactive process rooted in shared vision, commitment, trust, and openness between the actors.

In this book we will use the term "networked innovation" to describe the opening of innovation over company borders.

Networked innovation is defined as having the following characteristics:

(1) *the specific shared vision about targets of the collaboration,*
(2) *the collaboration process has several levels of openness and it is seldom open for everyone, although multiple actors are involved in the innovation,*
(3) *the collaboration covers both the knowledge transfer (co-operation) and the co-creation activity between actors,*
(4) *there is a contract either written or otherwise formed between the involved actors, and*
(5) *the co-ordination is based on both control-governance and self-organization.*

Within networked business environments and distributed knowledge sources firms must constantly look for and decide between different collaboration models in order to gain required IP, competences, and resources. The three main phases and focus areas of decision making about networked business and collaboration are:

(1) To analyse: why should a firm use in-house R&D, IP transaction, or co-creation within the innovation process?
(2) To define: how should a firm use in-house R&D, IP transaction, or co-creation within the innovation process?
(3) To choose: what is the appropriate model of in-house R&D, IP transaction, or co-creation a firm should use within the innovation process?

The phases and their basic elements are described in Fig. 3.2.

Firstly, a firm has to analyse external and internal drivers and motivation. This should be done based on a vision, an idea, or other development needs. IP strategy is an important guideline for decision making related to motivation and external and internal drivers of networked innovation. Chapters 6 and 7 go through the IP strategy and guidelines for making it. The analyses of the IP that is required, and the type of IP that it is

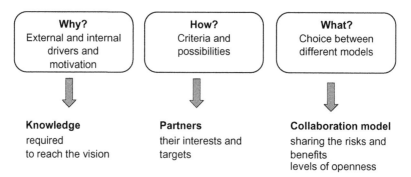

Fig. 3.2.   The main questions supporting the decision whether to use in-house R&D, IP transaction, or co-creation in innovation.

(well-documented, explicit knowledge (IPR), or tacit knowledge) influences the collaboration model, whether the IP is easily transferred or co-creation is required.

Secondly, the firm has to define the criteria and possibilities for accessing and acquiring the required knowledge, e.g. external knowledge sources and collaboration partners. This requires picturing the network and defining the firm's negotiation position, targets, and the interests of partners and connections between them. Naturally, the alignment of interests between actors related to targeted business and new tacit knowledge or IP needs to be analysed. Based on these definitions decision makers can also evaluate if they are willing and able to reward and motivate the partners with:

- Money
- Competences
- Reputation
- Collaboration and new relationships
- Rights to use the results under specified conditions (what are the conditions?)
- Ownership or joint ownership to potential results.

Thirdly, the firm has to choose the appropriate model of innovation initiative: in-house R&D, IP transaction, or co-creation. During the contracting process the firm has to negotiate with its network and partners about possible models of collaboration, sharing of IP, etc. This phase overlaps with the contracting process and its management. Chapter 5 considers the management of the network through contracting. Thereby, the network actors balance between formal management (contracts) and informal self-organization (trust, openness, and transparency). In this phase the collaboration model is constructed during the negotiation process and it describes:

- Structure of network (hub-spoke versus equal partners)
- Roles, responsibilities, rights and tasks of network actors
- Management of network
- Network's business model: benefits and cost sharing
- Renewal and development.

Determination of the collaboration model is always an iterative decision-making process between the firm and other network actors. The firm has to evaluate the strategic importance of networks and required IP. Furthermore, collaboration may influence other relationships and the firm's position within its networked business environment. These influences should also be evaluated when making a decision to open up the innovation processes of the firm.

In principle, the acquiring of explicit knowledge can be done more effectively in hub-spoke networks, whereas the access and co-creation of new knowledge necessitates more equal partnerships and horizontal co-operation (Valkokari *et al.*, 2012).

Chapter 4

Description of Collaboration Models in Networked Business

When studying collaborative practices in innovation between two or more actors (Paasi *et al.*, 2010), it was found that these practices generally involved either the co-creation of new knowledge (knowledge exploration) or transactions involving existing knowledge (exploitation of an earlier innovation outcome). Accordingly, the inter-organizational innovation relationships could be divided into two categories according to the intrinsic role of knowledge in these relationships:

- Co-creation networks
- Transaction networks.

In transaction networks (existing) knowledge is acquired through a transaction. The direction of the transaction may be from the outside to the inside, when a company is acquiring explicit knowledge (IP) from another actor, or from the inside to the outside, when a company is selling, licensing, or donating their own explicit knowledge (IP) to another actor. In co-creation networks the intention is to create new knowledge together with one or more actors. Sharing and generation of tacit knowledge plays an important role in the actual co-creation. Tacit knowledge is about understanding how to do things. Interaction and shared processes between the actors are required to create or transfer tacit knowledge. Often a prerequisite for this kind of collaboration is a limited access to the existing knowledge of each other. The levels of openness presented in Chapter 2 describe how this access can have several forms.

Table 4.1. Characteristic differences between co-creation and transaction networks.

	Transaction networks	Co-creation networks
Target of collaboration	Exploitation of existing knowledge	Exploration of new knowledge
Challenges of relationship and network orchestration	Participation interests according to appropriate business models	Participation and commitment based on shared interests
Nature of knowledge	Explicit knowledge, IP managed by formal methods (patents etc.)	Tacit knowledge during co-creation, possible explicit background IP, explicit outcome knowledge

The fundamental difference between the two types of open innovation networks is presented in Table 4.1. It is important to recognize that these models are complementary. Networked business development is a complex, iterative process that should be unfolded on multiple levels.

In both network types, collaborators have to make decisions about collaboration models and levels of openness (see also Chapter 2). To guarantee the appropriate levels of IP protection and innovativeness, the network actors negotiate during the contracting process about what is open or shared, with whom they co-operate, and how open the co-operation or collaboration is.

Knowledge Co-creation Networks

In the knowledge co-creation networks, the focus is on the creation of new knowledge and IP (i.e. knowledge exploration). Thereby, the joint targets of collaboration may often be fuzzy or even unknown at the beginning. All of this should be taken into account in contracting (see Chapter 9 for more details). The motivation behind the explorative collaboration in co-creation networks could be in:

- Searching of new business opportunities
- Improving operational efficiency of R&D
- Participating in industrial standardization
- Influencing the business environment and choices of other actors (for instance to increase own technology diffusion, market share, or brand value

- Interactive learning with no direct commercial targets (associations, benchmarking of best practices, etc.).

In the cases where the objectives of collaboration are related to learning, each of the network actors might have their own business objectives. There could also be direct joint commercial goals in the explorative collaboration which should be achieved by sharing and combining some special tacit knowledge of the actors, possibly with background IPR, and in this way to co-create new innovation. These closed co-creation networks are quite typically project-based initiatives, where the project plan defines the joint targets and tasks of the parties.

Co-creation networks can be classified at a high level into two types depending on whether all actors of the network are known or not. In closed networks, where all actors are known, the collaboration can furthermore be divided into bilateral, e.g. collaboration between two actors, or multilateral, when more than two actors are involved. This viewpoint is further discussed in Chapter 9 regarding the contracting process (see Fig. 9.1). High-level typology of co-creation networks is given in Fig. 4.1.

When the firm's own resources and knowledge base are not sufficient, *the closed models of co-creation* are often used to gain access to external knowledge sources. The closed collaboration models may facilitate knowledge sharing between involved actors better than open models, while it might be easier to create legal — or reputational — liabilities to others through formal agreements. In addition, when the co-ordination of open models turns out to be too complex or targets are too broad, the closed collaboration models may help to clarify the situation. Within closed co-creation networks there are still several levels of openness — transparency — regarding the joint innovation process (Chapter 2) defined by consortium agreements, when there are more than two collaborators. Therefore, a broad understanding about motivation and commitment of network actors, connected to contract design, is needed.

The most typical models of closed co-creation networks are research collaboration in academic projects and company-driven R&D projects. Typically, they differ from each other on initiator and focus. In academic projects the focus is on knowledge exploration and basic research and the research institutes are often initiators of projects. Academic projects often include public funding and they have to take into account the terms

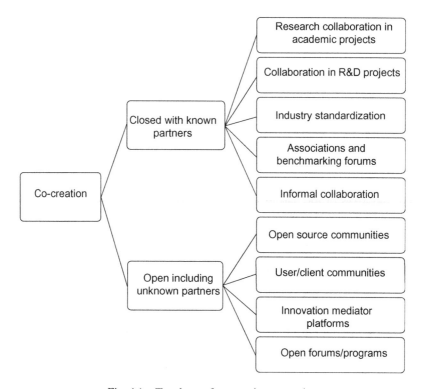

Fig. 4.1.   Typology of co-creation networks.

of a public financier. Company-driven R&D projects are launched and controlled by the firms, and they are closely connected to a firm's business development.

Industry standardization is a voluntary process of developing technical specifications based on a consensus among all interested parties. Within this process several conflicting interests may complicate the work. More informal models of co-creation are associations and benchmarking forums, where parties have their own business interests but would like to share some knowledge about best practices, thereby learning and gaining new perspectives from each other.

Open forms of co-creation networks typically involve several actors, with different degrees of involvement. Some actors are more tightly connected and committed to work than others. Accordingly, the chance that a single firm will have too much influence over the collaboration models is more unlikely when several actors are involved within open co-creation networks. Moreover, when the number of actors increases, the need for co-ordination mechanisms also increases. These forums and communities may exist for quite long periods of time, and their typically broad objectives allow also priorities, workplans, and activities to change over time as the original challenges are resolved, and new objectives may arise.

Open source communities are the most well-known model of collaborative peer-to-peer production. On the other hand, in Business-to-Customer collaboration the implication of user involvement in innovation has led to utilization of different user or client communities. Still in business-to-business collaboration business user communities are rare and collaboration is typically emphasized to closed networks with known parties. Innovation mediator platforms and open forums form a set of partially overlapping practices of open and networked innovation, from web-based portals operated by innovation intermediaries to intermediary activities in science and technology parks (Lopez and Vanhaverbeke, 2010).

In community-type open co-creation networks the collaboration model is formed by the involved actors, while in innovation mediator platforms and open forums the innovation inter-mediators have the main responsibility for controlling the innovation process. Still, within community-type collaboration arrangements there is also a core group, which is in charge of operations and forms the rules of the community. Membership of a network requires that actors endorse certain principles, like paying memberships fees or reporting on their activities or sharing their work to some extent.

Knowledge Transaction Networks

In the knowledge transaction networks the focus is on the existing knowledge and IP and the new business is built on that (i.e. the focus is on the exploitation of an earlier innovation outcome). Yet, the transaction networks only work when actors are able to define the required knowledge and agree on a transaction through formal business and contracting practices.

When an actor searches for the required knowledge and possible ways to access or acquire it, other players in the network that may have the knowledge will respond to the actions according to their own interests. A clear business value proposition, e.g. benefits related to actors' current business models, is typically a key success factor of co-operation within the transaction network. Furthermore, alignment of interests and agreement on the value of transacted IP are required between the actors of the network.

Transactions of knowledge may take place in the outbound direction (i.e. from inside to out) or in the inbound direction of the firm (i.e. from outside to in). The fundamental difference between outbound and inbound innovation processes within transaction networks is related to motives of knowledge transaction. Within inbound operations firms focus on the search for new IP, while within outbound operations the focus is on their present business opportunities. In the outbound viewpoint, a firm makes decisions related to the utilization of its IP. Quite naturally the IP strategy, which is considered in Chapters 6 and 7, should direct these decisions.

Similarly to the co-creation networks the transaction networks can also be classified according to whether all actors of the network are known or not. Both the outbound and inbound transactions may take place either in closed relationships with known actors or in open relationships involving unknown actors. In addition to these forms, cross-licensing is also defined as one co-operation model. A typology of knowledge transaction networks is shown in Fig. 4.2.

Within *the closed models of transaction networks* the contracting is typically bilateral. Thereby, the ownership of IP and confidentiality are unambiguously agreed. Within the closed models of transaction networks, a network actor influences only the actors with whom it does business directly, e.g. suppliers, partners, or customers.

The closed forms of transaction networks include buying or selling, licensing-in, licensing-out, different partnership models — like joint venture or strategic alliances — franchising, or other kinds of contracting for the knowledge sourcing. In buying or selling, a buying firm may obtain exclusive rights to the IP or, alternatively, the transaction may result in joint-ownership of the IP between the network actors. Joint ventures as well as strategic alliances have several types and operation models.

Furthermore, the closed IP transaction models could be accompanied by the transaction of tacit knowledge that is necessary for the utilization of the explicit IP through expert services (both rights and know-how) or through venturing or merging (both rights and business). In the latter case, the transaction relationship may often transform into a co-creation kind of relationship.

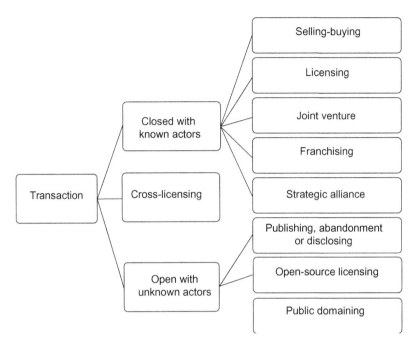

Fig. 4.2. Typology of transaction networks.

The *open forms of transaction networks* include abandonment of IP, disclosing or publishing of knowledge, and open-source licensing, and the utilization of public domain knowledge. Although direct business operations with other actors often do not take place in the open forms of transaction networks, decisions related to open knowledge should be carefully considered. Publishing of internal knowledge, for example, can be utilized as a method to affect the business environment and prevent competitors from applying formal protection to a similar kind of knowledge.

Chapter 5

Guide for Collaboration within Networked Business

Designing Networked Innovation and Business

The strategic approach to collaboration and network management seeks an answer especially to the "**how?**" question within networked innovation and business (Fig. 3.2). Thus, a networking strategy should be one element of a firm's business strategy in the networked business environment. Network strategy is strongly linked to a firm's business model, which describes the offering, the customers, required resources, value network (including suppliers), and earning logics. Technology strategy and/or IP strategy consider the value of knowledge and core-competences related to business areas and offerings.

Innovation and related business development or networking decisions, however, do not form a linear process. The phases form an iterative and multisided process (Fig. 5.1), where the decision and operations of one actor are always connected to other actors and their interests and actions. The management of networked business and innovation processes can be divided into company-level decision making and network-level negotiations.

This chapter includes tools for:

- Network analysis of actors and their roles (see the section "Network-level Negotiations and Contracting Capabilities of Firms")
- Choice of different collaboration models (see the section "Choice of Collaboration Models and Contracting")
- Relationship and interests analysis
- Network or relationships opportunities and risks-evaluation tool (both in the section "Alignment of Interest and Partner Selection").

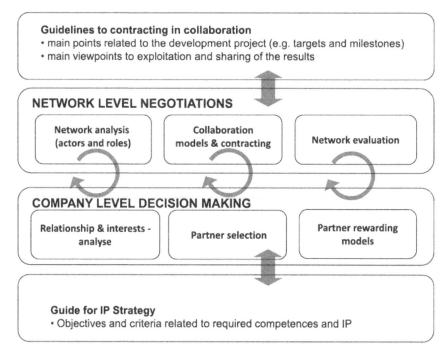

Fig. 5.1.   Guide for collaboration within networked business.

The tools will help a firm in choosing the most appropriate collaboration models, managing the network, and ensuring the commitment of partners. The classification of collaboration models was discussed earlier in Chapter 4. Partner rewarding models are covered in Chapter 7 and guidelines for contracts and contracting are discussed in the section "Network-level Negotiations and Contracting Capabilities of Firms" in this chapter, and in Chapter 9. Project management at network level is not covered in this workbook.

Picturing the network (network analysis) and defining a firm's negotiation position, targets, and interests of partners and connections between them are the starting points of the networking process. Within these analyses it is also important to recognize if there are missing links between actors (i.e. structural holes in the network). The missing links between network actors may indicate that there are knowledge gaps, which offer new business opportunities. The recognition of missing links in the network picture may help to find new partners for the co-creation of new knowledge or simply to re-use and utilize an idea from another business area.

Network analysis together with relationship and interests analyses are tools for configuring the network and deciding on the collaboration model. Based on these analyses, decision makers can also evaluate if they are willing and able to reward and motivate the partners. Hence, their own strategic considerations related to drivers and motivation to collaborate should be done before the start of the innovation work.

The strategic considerations about networks and other collaboration arrangements help to analyse the sources of competences and knowledge required to reach the business targets. The source of required knowledge can be internal or external or both. By using the following questions firms seek to find out *why they should collaborate* in innovation or why they shouldn't.

- How can we manage (foresee) the changes in our business environment, value network, or collaboration models?
- What are our (core) competences based on IP strategy? Are we able to describe the required new knowledge? How similar is the required knowledge to our core competences?
- What is the type of knowledge?
  ○ well-documented, explicit knowledge or IPR → easy to transfer
  ○ tacit knowledge, hard to transfer → co-creation required
- Is it possible to identify new crucial or essential knowledge (sources) based on IP strategy or structural holes in networked business environment? Would it create additional/new value to have external experts involved with idea enrichment or generation? How can we gain access to these external competences or experts?
- Which competences are we ready to share (and with whom)?
- How can we integrate internal and external competences? Are we able to utilize external knowledge?

During the steps towards networked innovation (see Fig. 5.2), a firm has to deal with explicit and tacit knowledge needs, the search for competencies, and the use of available IP. In order to foresee the development path of networked innovation, it is critical for the firm to understand the targets and motivation of each actor involved in the process. Then through negotiations

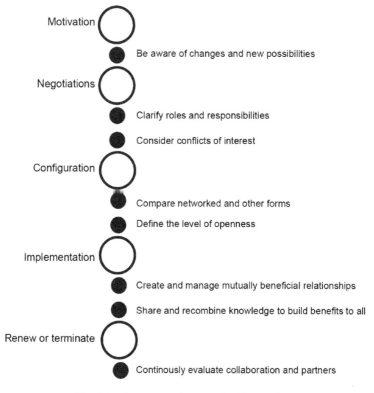

Motivation

Be aware of changes and new possibilities

Negotiations

Clarify roles and responsibilities

Consider conflicts of interest

Configuration

Compare networked and other forms

Define the level of openness

Implementation

Create and manage mutually beneficial relationships

Share and recombine knowledge to build benefits to all

Renew or terminate

Continuously evaluate collaboration and partners

Fig. 5.2.   Steps towards networked innovation.

the actors must clarify the roles and the responsibilities and consider conflicts of interest. Based on the negotiations and contracting, the actors are able to configure an appropriate form of networked innovation and commit to it. These conscious and transparent steps towards networked innovation enable actors to share and recombine knowledge to build unique intellectual properties to all network actors at the implementation and execution. Still, all involved actors should continuously evaluate collaboration and partners in order to decide whether to renew or terminate the co-operation.

Network management challenges and requirements for contracting are different in different networks. In co-creation networks, the co-operation is largely based on shared interests and trust between partners. Nevertheless, regardless of the trust between the partners, a formal contract protecting the rights and obligations of the parties, and extending the root of the collaboration from the initial personal relationships to a company-based level, should exist. It is important to realize that unwillingness to have a formal contract may indicate a reluctance interest to collaborate, rather than there being a high level of trust between the parties. In transaction networks the transferred knowledge is mainly explicit with clear formal protection. Accordingly, relationships and interaction are typically simple, and the collaboration is emphasized by formal contracts where safeguarding risk management plays an important role. The negotiations and contracting of networked business and innovation models is gathered in detail in the next section.

Network-level Negotiations and Contracting Capabilities of Firms

The main purpose of contracts is to bind the contracting parties. Since contracts are a means of private governance, the level and definitions of commitment are, however, connected with the motivations and business purposes of the parties. In transaction networks and closed co-operation, the protection of IP, confidentiality and clear rules for safeguarding from risks are crucial. Closed contracts are often bilateral. In open collaboration models, on the other hand, definition of purposes and commitment to co-operation are the key elements. Such contracts require flexibility (agility) in changed circumstances. Especially at the beginning of collaboration even the objectives of the contract may be unclear. Such incomplete and evolving contracts do not work without trust within collaboration parties. Contracts can also be supported by informal rules of the game or more specified rules of a community. The formal support of legal (public) governance weakens or gets less defined the more open the collaboration gets.

The network management is an iterative negotiation process with contracting. Thereby, the contracting considers different aspects of contracting capabilities: contract contents capability, contract process capability and network capabilities (see Fig. 5.3). Good contracting capabilities of an organization supports the interpreting of check-lists to be presented in Chapter 10, and implementing them in practice.

Although the contracting capabilities are here divided into three dimensions, in practice they should not be considered independently, since they all dynamically support each other. Network capabilities and the level of trust between the parties, as well as managing contracts as a process, have

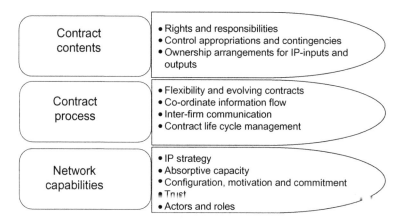

Fig. 5.3.   Contracting capabilities.

an impact in contract contents, whereas contract contents set the framework and the rules for collaboration.

Contract content capabilities concern management of appropriations, contingencies, ownership arrangements of IP inputs and outputs, and roles and responsibilities. Contracting process capabilities support in managing the information flow between the collaborating parties and to the outside of the network. Contracting process capability includes the capability to manage the whole innovation life cycle from planning and negotiations up to the post-contractual phase. Contracting process capabilities also provide a channel for intra- and inter-firm communication.

Network capabilities include building of trust, configuration, motivation, and commitment of parties, and managing openness in communication and dispute resolution. Network capabilities within parties are more important in the innovation design and development phases than in the commercialization phase, in which rights and responsibilities, risk management, chaining the liabilities and other hard elements of contract become more important.

In traditional contract law, the basic cornerstone is the *pacta sunt servanda* principle, which means that the contractual commitment binds the contracting parties as it was originally agreed. However in innovation networks, contracts require a more dynamic approach, since they develop gradually, may have been agreed as partially incomplete, and have to be specified or adjusted later on. Innovation contracts are evolving and flexibility is the rule in collaboration (Nystén-Haarala *et al.*, 2010). The exchanges in the innovation processes are often complex and, in order to respond to that, an opportunity to modify and develop the contract (an evolving contract) has to be introduced in the contracting process. Since traditional contract law regards contracts as static by nature and court ordering is not for adjusting evolving contracts, actors of the innovation process need to understand incomplete and evolving contracts as a means of private ordering. One goal in developing contracting capabilities is to create even more flexible ways to prevent problems from occurring and adjusting to changing circumstances and operational environments proactively.

The division between static and dynamic contracts is not relevant in all parts of a contract. Contractual arrangement can include both static and dynamic elements. Not all the contractual terms can be dynamic. The frame for collaboration has to be static and it also sets the rules for the dynamics. There are issues, such as liabilities, which typically stay as agreed in the first place. Dynamics are often introduced into contracts with relational methods, relying on good personal relationships between business partners or negotiation power and negotiation skills, and not exactly in contract clauses. Leaving flexibility only on a personal level, however, may lead to problems, for example, in the case of changes in personnel.

Consequently, developing only contract contents is not adequate, but the whole contracting process related to innovation has to be governed properly. Therefore, the contractual check-lists in this workbook (Chapter 10) are also done by considering the different aspects of contracting capabilities. The process has to be dynamic and agile in the changes of business environment. The contract document itself should not have an intrinsic value, but instead it should be an instrument supporting collaboration and parties to reach the shared goal. They can be seen as a formal frame for partners to execute the collaboration (Blomqvist *et al.*, 2008; Nystén-Haarala *et al.*, 2010). It is a way to formalize collaboration, introducing control and offering governance.

Analysis of Network Actors and Their Roles

The analysis of present and future networks is needed in order to identify the required partners for the co-creation or transaction of knowledge and for the

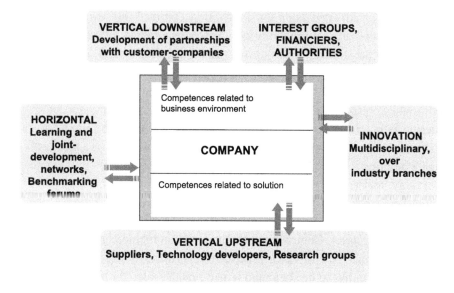

Fig. 5.4.   Network picture.

design of new business opportunities. Motives for knowledge co-creation or transaction are connected to a company's as well as its partners' present and future strategies and business models. Therefore, it is important to integrate the strategic reasoning of collaboration and IP management viewpoints.

The network picture (Fig. 5.4) is a starting point to represent actors, links, and resources, like IP. It is important to figure out a company's negotiation position related to possible partners. Furthermore, it is important to have a broader insight into networked business environment and figure out the actors who are not directly involved in the company's value creation process. For instance, exploring the business environment of a customer as well as defining customers of customers might offer new insights to the offering of a firm.

Typically the structure of the network can be divided into vertical customer–supplier collaboration, to horizontal collaboration with more equal partners, or to multidimensional collaboration consisting of both vertical and horizontal interactions. Strategic analysis based on the network picture also targets identification of the missing partnerships and structural holes of network, and thereby the potential for new business opportunities.

The possibilities for a firm to control negotiation and contracting processes are dependent on the network position, role, and business model of the firm. The vertical upstream business partner is a supplier, while the vertical downstream business partner is a customer or belongs to other interest groups. This difference has implications for the control that the company can exercise, for the nature of dependence in the relationship, and for the firm's ability to make changes in processes and systems in the interface.

The type of relationship between firms has important implications for how new knowledge is collected, shared, and used to improve existing products and to develop new products. The suppliers and customers have different capabilities as well as interests to contribute to the innovation process or business development. Anyhow, the relationships between suppliers and customers are typically long lasting and this relational embeddedness denotes strong ties and trust between the actors. That directs the actors to improve the prevailing dominant design and value network, and thereby the incremental innovations are more typical than radical.

Within the horizontal relationships, competences and willingness to contribute are even more heterogeneous. Although the companies typically are not willing to collaborate with competitors, because of similar experiences, knowledge phases and network positions, they could easily learn from each other and generate incremental innovations or broader solutions for their customers. Naturally, this kind of co-operative — e.g. concurrent competition and co-operation — relationship requires careful considerations about knowledge protection and sharing. On the other hand, horizontal relationships over industry branches, that bridge knowledge gaps and structural holes between the collaborators, are the most likely to generate radical innovations and new business opportunities.

The case example below illustrates the network picture of Solar Power Systems Ltd. This fictitious case example is utilized throughout the workbook in order to describe the meaning of tools.

Case example 1. Network picture of a system integrator (SOLAR POWER SYSTEMS LTD)

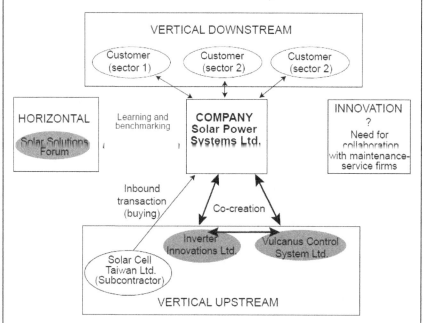

Solar Power Systems Ltd offers tailored industrial solutions to customers in several industrial sectors. Typical delivery of Solar Power Systems Ltd requires at least three suppliers and includes solar cells (Solar Cell Taiwan Ltd), an inverter (Inverter Innovations Ltd), and an automatic control system (Vulcanus Control Systems Ltd). The relationship with the supplier of solar cells (Solar Cell Taiwan Ltd) is on a subcontracting basis and based on tendering. Relationships with the two other main suppliers are strategic and tight because the tailoring of solutions requires that the parties open their knowledge and solutions to each other. Within deliveries close co-operation is needed also with customers. The customer relationships do not typically develop into partnerships as the deliveries are projects and Solar Power System Ltd does not offer maintenance services.

Solar Power Systems Ltd is an active member of "Solar Solutions" benchmarking forum, where its motivation for collaborating is related to

(*Continued*)

Case example 1. (*Continued*)
opportunity to gain new knowledge about technology development and best practices. Naturally, Solar Power Systems Ltd also wants to follow the actions of competitors and influence the diffusion of its own solutions by sharing the best practices within this group.

During the network analysis, Solar Power Systems Ltd realized that it would benefit from co-operation with service firms who take care of the maintenance of solar power systems. This collaboration would offer to Solar Power Systems Ltd deeper knowledge about needs of customers and understanding about the user requirements related to the solutions delivered by it and its partners.

Based on the network picture, a number of possible partners and their roles can be described. Table 5.1 presents the solid roles of different network actors. In practice, companies may have several overlapping roles within different business areas or based on the phase of innovation process or technology life cycle. The possible roles are: end customer or user, research partner, product or service company, suppliers under different models (like subcontractor, contract manufacturer, system supplier), system integrator, innovator, co-ordinator, and inter-mediator. Some of the roles, like research partner, innovator or co-ordinator, are typically identified in the design or development phases of innovation, while different supplier roles are more often involved in the offering phase of innovation.

The analysis of network roles supports the preparation for negotiations and the contracting process. Key issues related to contract content and process should be obtained during the analysis of network roles. Thus the analysis involves each actor's viewpoints on:

- Input, like competences and background knowledge, to the network
- Expectations about IP
- Needs for confidentiality
- Responsibilities
- Potential benefits, which can be utilized to rewarding and motivations
- Output, like rights related to collaboration outcome.

In order to support the formation of successful collaboration between members, companies must have clearly defined but different roles. For instance,

Table 5.1.   Actors of networked innovation: their roles and characteristic interests (related to IP management).

Role	Input: value and background knowledge	Responsibilities	Confidentiality	Motivation	Output: IP ownership and rights
End customer/ user	Knowledge about requirements, relevant processes and value networks	Describe the needs and requirements (define a pilot case)	Business and technology solutions	"First mover advantage" Rights to use the product or service	Rights to utilize the results (knowledge) in other similar cases
Product/ service company	Knowledge about business solution and customer needs, network connections	Develop, commercialize, offer products/services/ technology	Business and technology solutions	New approaches, solutions, knowledge about end user needs	Rights to utilize solution/ technology to offer products or services (in core areas IP ownership)
Subcontractor Contract manufac- turer	Easily purchased and specified product/solution	Offer products/services (transaction)		Sales and references	Rights to offer products to other customers
Supplier/ System Supplier	Product/solution connected to offering, complementary resources	Provide and develop (customize) product/service (co-creation)	Business and technology solutions and processes	New approaches, solutions, knowledge about customer and end user needs	Rights to utilize the technology/ solution to offer products or services in other business areas

(Continued)

Table 5.1. (*Continued*)

Role	Input: value and background knowledge	Responsibilities	Confidentiality	Motivation	Output: IP ownership and rights
System Integrator	Networking and integration competencies and position (close relationships to customer)	Integrate the products/services of several actors to customer solution	Customized business solutions and processes	New approaches, solutions, knowledge	Rights to offer the solution to other customers
Research partner	Research experience, knowledge about methods and tools	Create new solutions based on the research work	Theoretical frameworks, solutions and research networks	Funding to research, practical cases, business understanding	Intent to own IP in core research areas Utilize the results in further research projects
Innovator	Knowledge related to innovative solution	Offer innovative solutions and IP rights	Customized business solutions	Transaction of IP by selling, licensing, joint-venture, employment	IP ownership in order to offer IP to other customers (licensing agreements)
Co-ordinator Inter-mediator	Knowledge related to networked innovation and research projects	Co-ordinate collaboration and integrate solutions	Business solutions and research networks	Compensation about co-ordination work	No interest to own IP rights, interested to offer the co-ordination capacity to other actors

if several suppliers with similar resources participate in collaboration, the network co-ordinator (or core company) must clearly describe their positions and roles and make that transparent to the whole network. The difference can be found among others from production strategies, business models, or regional market positions. Analysis and discussions about the network roles also improve the commitment and motivation of partners, and may be utilized when planning the rewarding and earning logics of partners.

In case example 2 we illustrate Table 5.1 and describe the roles of Solar Power Systems Ltd and its partners in the offering network of Solar Power Systems.

Choice of Collaboration Models and Contracting

As described in the previous section, a network picture presents a firm's negotiation position related to possible partners. At first, analysis of network actors and their roles defines the motivation factors of the actors. After that discussions with possible partners may be needed in order to clear up in more detail their business logic, intentions, reasons for change, and expectations for the future. Concurrently, the choice between different collaboration models is done in the negotiation process within the members of the network.

The following questions try to define the criteria and possibilities to access or acquire the required knowledge, e.g. external knowledge sources and collaboration partners. By using these questions firms seek to find out *how to collaborate* in innovation and business development. The questions should be considered internally before starting the negotiations and contracting process with partners.

- From whom can we receive the required knowledge and competence (single or several sources)? How many partners should we commit?
- How can we utilize the knowledge and competences? Do we need to share our confidential knowledge with partners?
  o Learn
  o Buy
  o License
  o Take
- What is our negotiation position inside the network or in the networked business environment?
  o Are we able to describe interests of partners and the connections between them?

Case example 2. Actors and roles in the offering network of Solar Power Systems Ltd.

Actor and role	Input: value and background information	IP ownership	Confidentiality	Responsibilities	Rewarding and motivations	Output: rights related to the collaboration outcome
End customer	Tacit knowledge about requirements and relevant processes	Ownership of tailored solution	Tacit knowledge about business and technology solutions	Describe the needs and requirements	Need for tailored solution	No rights to utilize the solution elsewhere
Solar Power Systems (System Integrator)	Networking and integration competencies and position	Solution is based on both tacit knowledge and IP	Tacit knowledge about customized business solutions and processes	Integrate the products and competences of network actors to customer solution	Compensation about integration work => business model based on the value added	Offer the solution to other customers (in co-operation with network actors)
Inverter Innovation and Vulcanus Control Systems (System Suppliers)	Solution connected to offering, complementary resources	Product/ solution owner	Tacit knowledge about business solutions and processes	Provide and develop (customize) product (co-creation)	New approaches, solutions, knowledge about end user needs	Utilize the technology/ solution to offer solutions in other business areas
Solar Cell Taiwan (Subcontractor)	Easily purchased and specified prod-uct/solution	Product/service/ capacity owner	Limitations based on the competitive situation	Offer products/ services (transaction)	Sales and references	Offer products to other customers

- o What are the benefits of collaboration for us or for our partners?
- o Will the partners (or their targets) harm or improve our position?
- o Should we change the structure of existing value chain?
- How should we reward and motivate the partners?

- o Money
- o Competences
- o Reputation
- o Rights to use the results under specified conditions => what are the conditions?
- o Ownership or joint ownership to potential results

- How can we utilize and reward internal knowledge sources (employment agreement on employee inventions, partnership management)?

Through network analysis a company can define an innovation network and it can structure its own role, position, negotiation power, and credibility in its business environment. Network typologies (presented in Chapter 4) illustrate the choice of different collaboration models on a general level, while the contractual check-list supports companies to define the rules of collaboration in detail. Furthermore, the relationships and interests tool (see the next section of this chapter) can be utilized in order to define the alignment of interests between the actors who will be involved in the collaboration and offering of targeted business solutions.

The questions below help companies to choose and negotiate about an appropriate collaboration model. By using these "**what**" questions firms seek out aspects related to the potential collaboration (Fig. 3.2).

- What is the most effective and fastest co-operation model? Which competences are we ready to share (and the partners are willing and able to utilize)?
- What is the business value of associated IP or knowledge? How can our valuable knowledge be protected? How do we ensure that confidential knowledge is not leaked out to potential competitors? => business models: sharing of costs and benefits.
- How should we influence, motivate, and convince the partners?
- How will the co-operation function (based on the earlier experiences, expectations and reputation of partners)?
- How can we collect ideas from collaborators or other actors?

- How does this collaboration affect other networks (or business areas and IP's/competences related to these) of which we utilize or take part? => strategic importance of collaboration.
- What kind of agreements about the prohibition of competition are needed?

Contracts play different roles in the exploration and exploitation phases of innovation. Contracts regarding the research and development work have different aims than contracts in the commercialization of innovation outcome. Accordingly, different contractual functions and capabilities have to be taken into consideration in these phases. As described in Chapter 2, collaboration models and contracts (or other rules and norms shared between the participants) can include different levels of openness. At the exploration phase of innovation, where the results of collaboration cannot be foreseen, the companies often utilize more open collaboration models than in the knowledge exploitation phase, where participants want to ensure their own business opportunities and their position in the value network related to created or transacted IP by using a more closed model of collaboration.

Alignment of Interest and Partner Selection

Based on earlier collaboration experiences, analyses of network roles, and first discussions, the alignment of interests between the actors can be analysed at the network level (Fig. 5.5). The relationship and interests analysis describes the situation in bilateral relationships between the core firm and its partners in the innovation network.

Relationship types are classified into simple relationships, which are typical in transaction networks, and complex relationships, which stand for frequent interaction at several levels of organizations. The horizontal axis defines what kind of co-operation is required in order to gain the objectives of networking. The levels of openness described already in Chapter 2 can also be utilized to analyse the complexity of relationships.

The vertical axis describes how well the interests of network actors are aligned. The actors should consider if the interests of all participants are aligned to each other and to the joint objectives of collaboration. When considering the alignment of interests, the analysis can be started from the network position, role, and business model of partners (see the section "Analysis of Network Actors and their Roles" in this chapter). It seeks out

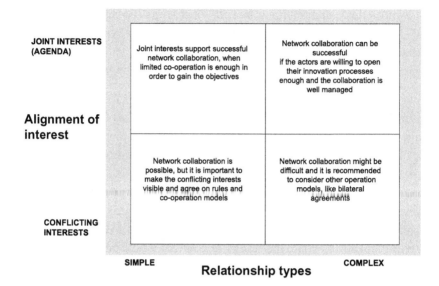

Fig. 5.5.   Relationship and interests analysis.

potential conflicting interests related to the actual target of collaboration or that may emerge due to partners' other business areas, collaboration, or ownerships. In the process of partner selection, it is important also to consider conflicting interests between the potential partner firms, although the analysis does not directly describe these conflicts.

Relationships with new partners are often complex. Long-lasting co-operation derives from complex relationships as co-operation is frequent and done at several levels of organizations. At the same time, conflicting interests between partners may also emerge. Changes in strategy or business models of partners may lead to conflicting interests between the partners and, therefore, it is important to evaluate the network relationships systematically.

When the interests of actors in the network are well aligned, the success of work depends much on the need of willingness of the actors to open their innovation process and knowledge to the other actors in the networks. If all that is required for open innovation is simple, transactional work between some or all of the actors, then the collaboration should be straightforward. However, if the collaboration is complex, and it is essential that the innovation process is open and knowledge is shared, then this need and this agenda of openness should be clearly communicated to each network actor, and the collaboration should be well managed during the whole work.

Conflicting interests between some of the network actors may not hinder successful collaboration in an innovation network, but they always require some co-ordination in order to manage the potential problem. If the relationships between actors with conflicting interests are simple, it may be adequate to make the conflicting interests visible and agree separately on rules and co-operation models. If the relationships, however, need to be complex, a networked operation may not be a feasible solution and one should consider, for example, doing the innovation work by using bilateral agreements. It may also be useful to analyse opportunities and risks related to the collaboration in more detail before entering into an agreement.

Successful collaboration requires openness and transparency of targets between the collaborators. In order to develop the collaborative relationships, it is recommended that the evaluation of network relationships is kept open to collaboration partners, at least to some extent. Furthermore, concrete, shared, and, where possible, measurable targets will support partners' motivation and commitment to participate in collaboration.

Case example 3 represents the relationship and interest analysis between Solar Power Systems Ltd and its partners.

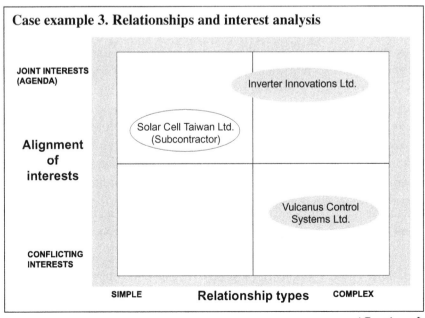

Case example 3. Relationships and interest analysis

JOINT INTERESTS (AGENDA)

Alignment of interests

Inverter Innovations Ltd.

Solar Cell Taiwan Ltd. (Subcontractor)

Vulcanus Control Systems Ltd.

CONFLICTING INTERESTS

SIMPLE   **Relationship types**   COMPLEX

(Continued)

Case example 3. (*Continued*)

Solar Power Systems Ltd has a long experience of collaboration with its system suppliers Inverter Innovations and Vulcanus Control Systems Ltd. They have joint interests through their tailored offerings. However, Vulcanus Control Systems Ltd has renewed its strategy to broaden the utilization of their control system solutions in a way that may negatively influence the market position of Solar Power Systems Ltd, and this leads to partly conflicting interests between Vulcanus and Solar Power System.

Solar Power Systems Ltd has to evaluate opportunities and risks related to the collaboration with Zeus Control Systems in more detail before making a decision about whether to continue the collaboration or not.

The relationship with Solar Cell Taiwan Ltd is simple and based on the clear order-delivery process.

Depending on the results of relationships and interests analysis or other strategic considerations, a need to evaluate a certain relationship and its opportunities and risks in more detail may emerge. Case example 4 represents tools for an opportunity and risk evaluation. Partner selection is typically a situation where it may be necessary to evaluate the opportunities and risks of potential collaboration.

A final decision related to the partner selection is done through the negotiating process with potential partners. Former experiences and reputation of possible partners as well as alignment of interests are important factors. Different tools like SWOT-analysis and the evaluation of opportunities and risks will give valuable information for the decision making. Basically, it is a question of strategic thinking and analysis where it is essential to identify present and future business opportunities and risks from the viewpoints of all collaborators. These considerations should be linked to IP strategies of participants (to be discussed in the next chapters), and for example to the rewarding of partners (see the section "Questions Regarding Actions and Decisions on Co-creation-type Networks" in Chapter 7).

Case example 4. Evaluation of opportunities and risks

Due to the partly conflicting interests with Vulcanus Control Systems Ltd, Solar Power Systems Ltd wanted to evaluate the opportunities and

(*Continued*)

Case example 4. (*Continued*)

risks of collaboration in more detail. The target is to clear out if a closer strategic co-operation within certain customer sectors could improve the future competitiveness of both the Vulcanus Control Systems Ltd and Solar Power Systems Ltd.

Solar Power Systems Ltd recognized several opportunities and risks with collaboration for both companies. Opportunities were related to: new business potential; improved market potential; the opportunity for companies to utilize external resources; contact with new partners; learning new ways and methods for co-operation; applying new technological knowledge about each other's solution; and potential for creating new IP based on shared knowledge.

Opportunities		
Business potential	4	Opportunity for new or replacement business potential due to project results
Market position	10	Opportunity for improved market position (e.g. market share or size) due to project results
External resources	10	Ability to utilize external network resources in own business
New partners	10	Opportunity to create new partnerships due to collaboration
Learning from collaboration	3	Ability to learn new ways and methods of collaborating as a result of collaboration
Technological knowledge	4	Ability to improve technological know-how as a result of the collaboration
New IPR	1	Potential for creating new intellectual property for the company from the project results
Average	**6.6**	

Risks of collaboration were related to: the business potential of the new solution; markets; the loss of key knowledge or IP during collaboration; not having adequate knowledge and competences to reach the targets; and not reaching the objective due to, e.g. technological challenges, and network risks, such as changes to targets or even changes of ownership.

(*Continued*)

Case example 4. (*Continued*)

Risks

Business risk	5	Risk that the developed solution is not relevant for the target markets
Network risk	3	Risk of changes in e.g. partner interests or ownership during the product or service life cycle
Knowledge risk	6	Risk of losing key knowledge or IPR to competitors during development project
Competence risk	1	Risk of not having adequate knowledge to reach the target during development project
Target risk	4	Risk of not reaching the objective due e.g. technological challenges during development project
Network risk	1	Risk of challenges in e.g. partner interests or ownership during development project
Average	**3.3**	

The opportunities and risk from the viewpoints of both Solar Power Systems Ltd and Vulcanus Control Systems Ltd were aggregated. The evaluation shows that generated business idea is more appropriate for Solar Power Systems Ltd than to Vulcanus Control Systems Ltd as the opportunities are higher and the risks lower. Although the difference is not remarkable, it is important to analyse the factors in detail in order to understand the motivation and possible business models for both.

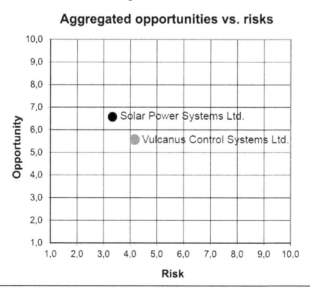

Aggregated opportunities vs. risks

(*Continued*)

Case example 4. (*Continued*)
The opportunities and risks evaluation supports the alternative that Solar Power Systems Ltd would start discussions with Vulcanus Control Systems Ltd for a closer strategic collaboration.

Business opportunities and risks are different in different phases of innovation, and their evaluation is more challenging in the knowledge exploration than in the exploitation phase. The network structure and situation also have an influence on the business opportunities and risks. If the collaboration targets a business solution which replaces an existing value network, the risks are typically high but more easily defined, especially when the collaborators already have a market position, experiences about comparable solutions, and relevant IP. In the case of radical innovation or a radically different business model that requires the construction of a new value network, the realization as well as commercialization of innovation will take more time and the risks are typically higher and harder to foresee.

The increased complexity of products and services has also led to a situation where their value is linked to other products or services. Thus, it is important to consider and analyse strategically the networked business environment also in those cases where the companies decide not to utilize networked innovation processes. There are — and will be — situations where the closed in-house innovation is the most appropriate choice, for instance due to the strategic importance of IP, business models and network positions of actors or when the required knowledge already exists in-house.

Part III

IP STRATEGY

Networked Business
• Description of collaboration
  models
• Guide for collaboration

IP Strategy
• Description of IP strategy
• Guide for collaboration

Practices & Actions
• Methods of knowledge protection
• Contracting process
• Contractual check-lists
• Glossary

Chapter 6

Description of IP Strategy

In many firms, IP strategy means, in practice, the same as patent strategy. In this view, IP strategy in a company would set the internal guidelines on the protection and use of such technologies that fulfil the criteria for patentability. Knowledge which is not able to be protected under prevailing patent legislation or for which patenting might not offer suitable benefits is not usually covered in this type of IP strategy — even though the knowledge itself could be of high importance to the company.

In the context of open and networked innovation, however, IP strategy should have a broader meaning. In this context, IP strategy should cover all controllable knowledge that is important for a firm. This entails knowledge of different levels of formality and codification. Some of that might be controlled through formal legal mechanisms, some through contracts between companies, and some through companies' internal practices and procedures. And the IP strategy is not only about the protection of knowledge; it is also about controlled sharing of knowledge. Accordingly, *IP strategy could be defined as the following*:

> *IP strategy is a company's awareness about what knowledge is important for the company and how the IP should be protected, managed, or shared in order to support the business model and business strategy of the company.*
>
> *IP strategy focuses both on knowledge that can be controlled with formal intellectual property laws, and also knowledge and other intangible resources whose use may be controlled by contracts, policies, organization and process routines and norms, both physically and technically.*

In the definition, IP strategy is tightly linked to business strategy. Without a well-defined idea of where the company's sustainable competitive advantage comes from, it is difficult to set guidelines for managing such knowledge that supports this competitive advantage.

The main goals of a successful IP strategy are:

- To link a company's own competences and knowledge with the objectives of business and technology strategies
- To identify and make visible their own IP and to identify the relevant IP of others
- To improve the valuation of IP and to enable the comparison of their own IP against strategic objectives
- To enable systematic management of IP.

The role of IP strategy in a company can be seen by viewing the continuum from the company's high-level IP policies to individual IP decisions, as depicted in Fig. 6.1. The IP management is divided into three levels, labelled here as IP strategy, IP practices, and IP actions. IP strategy sets the broad guidelines for the objectives and use of IP in each market area and technological area that is important for the company. In other words, IP strategy should describe what parts of intellectual property of the company are needed and how is it going to be used in each market area to maintain

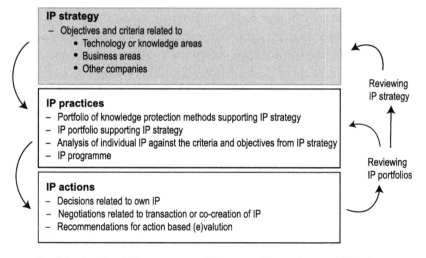

Fig. 6.1.   Levels of IP management: IP strategy, IP practices, and IP actions.

competitiveness. IP strategy should specify the objectives for the use of IP in each area and criteria against which these objectives can be measured. The links to other companies' IP and the rationales for the potential use of complementary IP of other companies should also be described.

Based on the high-level guidelines, a suitable portfolio of IP protection methods is chosen for each area. Individual IP decisions should be made based on the defined higher-level objectives rather than on an *ad hoc* basis. Sometimes this may mean opening and sharing of IP with other actors in a controlled manner to support innovation and new business development actions of the firm. Here an IP strategy should also state what IP the firm can open and share with others (and with whom and how) and what IP it cannot. Thus, in our view, IP strategy should be able to assist in the case-specific decision making and also be broader than merely a description of the company's processes and responsibilities of decision making related to IP management. This part of IP strategy is labelled in the figure as "IP programme".

Another way of approaching IP strategy is to view its role in relation to a company's technology and business strategies. This is illustrated in Fig. 6.2. For a technology-oriented company, the key knowledge is often highly technology based. In these cases, IP strategy is often a subset of the company's technology strategy, defining principles of protection of key technologies for the company. Similarly, technology strategy constitutes one, often critical, part of the overall business strategy of the technology company. In contrast, for a non-technology-oriented company, such as a

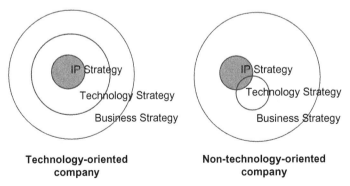

Fig. 6.2. Relationship between business strategy, technology strategy, and IP strategy (modified from van Wijk, 2005).

content provider, IP strategy may be completely distinct from the technology strategy, as the key know-how and competitive advantage of the company is not technology related.

Traditionally the alignment of IP, technology, and business strategies has meant intensive closed own development work and patent protection of key technologies. Nowadays, when companies open their innovation, the ways in which the technology strategy is realized (in a technology-oriented company) using the IP strategy are more diverse than in the past. We have defined the IP strategy, very broadly, as a company's awareness of the knowledge that is important for the company, and how IP should be protected, managed, or shared to support the company's business model and business strategy. It is important to realize, however, that technology strategy goes well beyond the traditional IP protection of key technologies. As an example, for one IT company the competitive advantage of the business is reached through its own protected software. For another the competitive advantage of the business may be reached through interactive utilization of knowledge in open source communities. In the former case, the IP strategy should say what technology (software) should be protected and how. In the latter case, the IP strategy should give strategic principles and practices about how the company operates interactively in open source communities.

Although we have here underlined the relationships and alignment between business, technology, and IP strategies, we do not consider in this workbook the making of business and technology strategies but focus on giving guidelines for making an IP strategy by assuming that the business technology strategies exists or are in progress in parallel with the IP strategy.

Chapter 7

Guide for Making IP Strategy

The main task of an IP strategy is to describe the approaches and methods used by the company's IP to support the business strategy and business models. More specifically, a company's IP strategy should give answers to the following:

- What to protect, and why
- What not to protect, i.e. what to share, and why
- How to protect
- How to share in a controlled manner
- How to manage
- How could others' IP support our business strategy and business models?

As in strategy work in general, answers to the key questions should be searched for by having multiple viewpoints of the situation. In this chapter we give a set of tools that will support the formation of such a viewpoint. Furthermore, we give an architecture for the documentation of IP strategy (see the section "IP Strategy Documentation").

Comparison of IP Portfolio against Offerings

One way to approach the drafting of IP strategy is to start with a comparison between the company's offerings and the business models, and the current scope of knowledge protection methods used in offerings, as illustrated in Fig. 7.1. The figure compares the scope of a company's current or future business or technological offerings (point 1 in the figure and in the list below) against the scope of the current IP portfolio (point 2 in the figure).

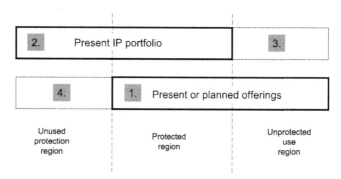

Fig. 7.1. Analysis of present IP portfolio against present offerings (modified from Chesbrough, 2006b).

Of these, we identified the areas which are not protected but still offered (point 3) and the areas in which IP assets exist but are not utilized.

1. What is offered or planned to be offered within each business or technology area (based on business or technology strategy)?

   - Scope of offering in each area
   - Objective for IP in that area (see the next section of this chapter)

2. What is the coverage of current IP with respect to that offering?

   - Listing of company's IPR relevant to that area
   - Listing of other IP relevant to that area
   - Listing of currently in-licensed IP in that area

3. What needs to be done with IP now and in the future to match the current and planned offerings?

   - What kind of IP do we need to develop ourselves?
   - What kind of IP of other companies can we utilize (or need to utilize) to reach the stated objective?

4. How could the IP that we are not planning to use in our offerings be utilized?

   - What IP can be divested out from?
   - What part of unused IP could be utilized by other companies?

Case example 5. Comparison of current and future offerings against the IP assets of Solar Power Systems Ltd.

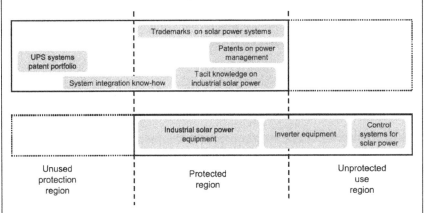

The offerings of Solar Power Systems Ltd include industrial solar power equipment, inverter equipment, and IT control systems for solar power systems. Their IP assets include a few patents of algorithms related to power management. They have a strong trademark portfolio on industrial solar power systems to protect their business. In addition, they also own a portfolio of patents related to uninterruptible power supply (UPS) systems from their discontinued businesses. In addition to these formal IP protection methods, Solar Power Systems also has considerable tacit knowledge on industrial solar power to complement their trademarks and on efficient implementation of solar power systems.

The IP of Solar Power Systems Ltd on solar power systems and power management is well utilized in their business. The actual solar cells are off-the-shelf equipment that Solar Power Systems buys from markets (mainly from Solar Cell Taiwan Ltd) and, from the viewpoint of Solar Power Systems, one may say that the IP of solar cells is not an issue. On the area of control systems and inverter equipment, Solar Power Systems does not own the necessary IP that would be needed for the complete systems and, therefore, Solar Power Systems has close collaboration with Vulcanus Control Systems Ltd and Inverter Innovations Ltd on projects that require their knowledge. On the other hand, the patent portfolio of Solar Power Systems Ltd on UPS systems is not linked to any current offerings and thus they seek to find a partner to capture value from that part of the IP portfolio through licensing, sale, or joint venture.

Sources of Value for IP

To assess the value of different IP assets of the company, the IP strategy would first need to identify the source of value that is sought from that IP. Depending on the planned use of IP, the value might be realized in different ways. The value may result directly from, e.g. increased cash flows, or more indirectly from, e.g. improved competitive position that the IP gives. One possible categorization of the different sources of value for IP is given below.

- **Freedom of Action (FA)**

The effect of the patent or other IP on the ability to conduct business in strategically important markets without the risk (or with reduced risk) of being sued for infringement.

- **Product Differentiation (PD)**

Price premium or increased sales resulting from unique product features (or unique features of the offering in general) attributable to the IP.

- **Licensing Revenue (LR)**

Additional revenue from licensing the patented technology for use in other companies or favourable terms attributable to the IP in cross-licensing agreements with key technology holders.

- **Operational Efficiency (OE)**

Reduced costs resulting from using the IP in a company's own production process.

- **Influence in Business Environment (IBE)**

Ability to affect the future markets for technology and steer technological development in a favourable direction with the IP.

- **Increase in Brand Value (IBV)**

Increased marketing or brand value of the company or its attractiveness as an employer or partner, attributable to the IP.

Fig. 7.2.   Different objectives of IP and the corresponding source of value.

Figure 7.2 illustrates these sources of value for IP. Protected knowledge that improves efficiency inside the company may result in reduced operating costs for the company. Licensed or contracted knowledge can yield profitable agreements or additional cash flow from other market participants. Finally, the return from unique protected product features usually come in the form of additional revenue from the product markets. Brand value, freedom of action value, and influence value can have an impact on any of these, depending on the situation.

Linking Business and Technology Strategies with IP Strategy

Another way of drafting or reviewing IP strategy starts from a consideration of links between the business areas or business models important to the company and the different key technological areas. One would first establish a list of key business models together with a motivation or objective for each of them (these should already have been defined in the company's business strategy).

- What are the main technological areas utilized by the company currently or in the future? What additional competences or IP needs to be developed or acquired?

- What are the life cycle phases of the identified technological areas? Which are in their infancy, which are being developed, and which are mature technologies?
- What does the current IP portfolio for the technological areas look like? What are current areas of strong and weak IP, respectively?
- Who are the other relevant IP owners in the technological areas? What do their IP portfolios look like?
- Which companies own valuable complementary IP? With whom can we collaborate? Which companies offer substitute or competitive IP to our own?

Next, one would make a similar list of main technology areas together with motivations as to why this area is important to the company (these are hopefully already established in the company technology strategy). Note that technology areas can in this context also refer to more generic areas of knowledge that are of major importance to the company, if the company is non-technology-oriented.

- What is the size and structure of the relevant market areas? Which are large, and which are small? Which of them are broad markets with many customers, and which are specialized niche markets with few major customers?
- What are the life cycle phases of potential target markets? Which are emerging, which are rapidly growing, and which are declining?
- Who are the other companies operating in our relevant market areas? With whom can we potentially collaborate? Who are our main competitors? What is our competitive strength in each market area? How well can our competitive position be protected with IP?
- How technology-intensive are the different market areas? What technology is needed to serve customers in each market segment? How do they fit into our own IP? What competences need to be developed or acquired?

Each business model of a company typically applies one or several technologies. Or conversely, each technology is utilized in one or more business models. Non-technology oriented companies may here speak about knowledge areas instead of technologies. IP strategy should define how each "link" between technology areas and business areas should be managed and the corresponding tools or portfolio of protection methods that are used to reach this objective (see the list in the previous section). In other words, just obtaining IP protection for a given knowledge asset does not necessarily yield any value for the company without defining how, where, and why that protection is going to be used. Moreover, IP strategy should help to define in which business or technology areas a company needs technology from outside, is ready to transfer technology outside, or seeks collaboration with outside partners.

The approach is presented in Fig. 7.3 below. Boxes at the top represent the company's business areas and boxes in the middle represent technology areas in which the company has knowledge that can be protected. Boxes below the technology areas represent the scope of IP strategy, i.e. the portfolio of protection methods for each technology area. The lines represent the identified links between the technology and business areas. Each link is marked with the methods for how the corresponding IP is utilized in the business area and what the objectives are for IP in that area.

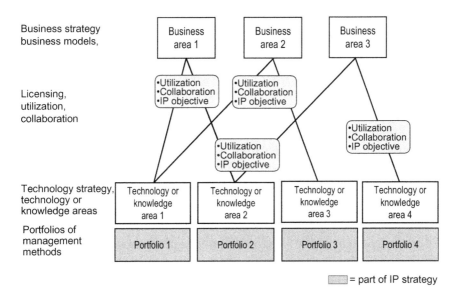

Fig. 7.3. Linking business and technology strategies with IP strategy.

Case example 6. Linking business and technology strategies with IP strategy

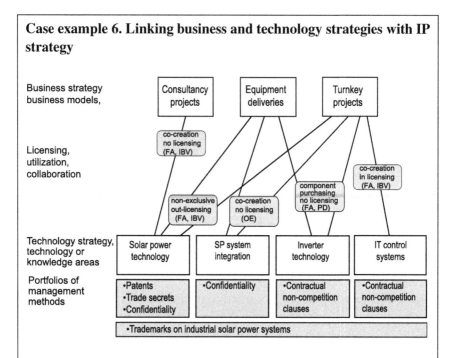

Solar Power Systems Ltd employs three main business models: (i) consultancy projects offering the know-how of Solar Power Systems to examine the potential for the use of industrial solar power technology in the customer environment; (ii) pure equipment deliveries of industrial solar power technology for advanced customers; and (iii) fully tailored turnkey projects for installing and integrating solar power systems to a specific customer application. The technology areas that they utilize in these fields of business consist of: (i) specialized industrial solar power technology, protected by patents and trade secrets; and (ii) system integration know-how in the form of tacit knowledge. Additionally, Solar Power Systems needs the intellectual property from the fields of (iii) inverter technologies and (iv) IT control systems, provided by Inverter Innovations Ltd and Vulcanus Control Systems Ltd, respectively. These are not owned by Solar Power Systems but a degree of protection for those technologies is given by contractual non-competition clauses with the two companies that prevent the sales of the utilized technologies to the competitors of

(Continued)

Case example 6. (*Continued*)

Solar Power Systems. Furthermore, Solar Power Systems owns a strong portfolio of widely recognized trademarks on industrial power systems products.

According to its IP strategy, Solar Power Systems has established the following practices to support its business strategy in the three business areas. Firstly, in the consultancy projects, they utilize their proprietary tacit know-how (FA) and brand image (IBV) in the field of solar power systems technology to gain a competitive advantage against other providers of consultancy services. However, no licensing agreements on the actual use of that technology are made with the customer so that the consultancy business does not cannibalize their other business areas. Secondly, in the equipment delivery area, the proprietary solar power technology is licensed out (LR) to the customer together with the physical products and the proprietary components from Inverter Innovations (PD). Solar Power Systems use their tacit knowledge of system integration in carrying out the projects efficiently (OE). Finally, in the turnkey project deliveries, they also need the licences from Vulcanus Control Systems Ltd for their control system software product, as well as the knowledge of Vulcanus for the customization integration of the software product for the specific customer application (FA, PD).

IP Strategy Documentation

Drafting of the company IP strategy should conclude with clear documentation. IP strategy documentation could consist of two parts: one describing the content and the objectives of IP protection and the methods used in different market areas or business models, as delineated in the previous sections; and another document describing the process-related issues, responsibilities, and policies of IP management, labelled here as "IP programme".

IP strategy:

- Chosen technology or market areas
- Objectives of company IP in those areas
- Chosen portfolio of IP protection (management) methods in each of areas

IP programme:

- IP process description
- Reviewing IP assets
- Monitoring of outside IP
- Confidentiality policy
- Employee education

The process description of the decision making regarding IP assets is a major part of the IP programme (in many companies this is the sole content of IP strategy). This part should define the roles and responsibilities of the company employees regarding execution and handling of IPs as well as the reviewing and decision-making mechanisms that are put in place for both internal and external IP assets. For internal assets, the focus should be on the continuity and systemizing of the process. This includes, e.g. that the justifications and the assumptions for the individual decisions made are clearly stated and based on the objectives of IP strategy so that they can be more easily reviewed later on, when new information has been obtained. For outside IP assets, the most systematic monitoring should naturally be focused on the identified technology areas of the company, as well as on the development of IP by other key players in the company's main business areas.

Similarly, the IP programme should establish and communicate the confidentiality policies of the company. In addition to non-disclosure agreements and other contractual measures to control diffusion of private information, clear guidelines should be set on the types of information that the company employees are authorized to share with their outside partners. There is naturally a trade-off between a strict confidentiality policy on one hand and, on the other hand, the potential new innovations that might result from free flow of ideas between the employees of the company and its outside partners. It should be noted that an effective IP strategy can also be a source of competitive advantage or contain critically important information for the company and thus its confidentiality should be discussed as well. The confidentiality policy should also give the employees of the company guidelines for their actions on social media. The policy should guide what they can write on social media and what they cannot in issues related to their work, and in which role they should be in social media. It is important to establish, for example, who has the right to use "the company's voice" on social media. There may be named persons whose job role includes the use of social media to support the business targets of the company. The policy should also guide employees on the situations in which they represent the company in social media as employees and are therefore using the company's voice, and the situations in which they should use social media as private persons.

Finally, the most important aspects of the management of the company's IP need to be effectively communicated to the employees, along with their rationales. This is especially important regarding the informal protection methods as their potential efficiency does not result from either IP legislation or contractual agreements but rather from the actions of the individual company employees.

Controlled Sharing of IP

IP strategy is not just about choosing areas that need intellectual property protection and the methods through which that protection is obtained. The main benefits for a company might not result from the use of IP by the company itself, but rather from the use of IP by its collaboration partners or third parties, which seems especially topical in the open and networked innovation context. For example, many successful software companies are interactively utilizing open source communities in their development process. So successful business is not only restricted to cases where companies manage to keep the essential parts of their code base proprietary. A company utilizing an open source approach could choose to share all the essential software parts of their offering while at the same time having the best possible resources in-house to utilize the benefits that come from open source development work.

Thus, it is important to consider the benefits and trade-offs in deciding on how tight a control the company wants to have over its IP rights. In its most basic form, the trade-off is between no sharing, or a low level of sharing of IP rights on one hand, which makes it possible to get, e.g. direct cash flow income from out-licensing agreements, and a higher level of sharing on, and lower control over, IP on the other hand, which enables wider use of IP and, e.g. potential indirect income through favourable development and improved positioning in the market environment. A challenge that makes this trade-off difficult to analyse is that the indirect benefits from the more open use of IP through collaboration with partners and other stakeholders is often difficult to quantify even though those benefits might be significant. On the other hand, the potential direct cash flow payments from closed licensing practices are often more readily quantified as are the costs that have been incurred in developing those competences and IP rights.

As discussed above in the section "Sources of Value for IP", a company might have several ways to utilize and benefit from the different parts of its IP portfolio. Similarly, the degree of sharing of these rights might vary between the different IP assets that the company has. One way to visualize the degrees of control that a company plans to have over its IP areas and the level of sharing in these is to plot the IP areas against the different degrees of openness, which were introduced in Chapter 2 (see Tables 2.1 and 2.2). To illustrate this, we have depicted in Fig. 7.4 the sources of value against the levels of openness.

In the figure, we have used the same categorization for the degrees of openness as in Table 2.1, from closed to public. Additionally, the vertical axis shows the degree to which the IP is thought to be used either internally by the company or externally by outsiders.

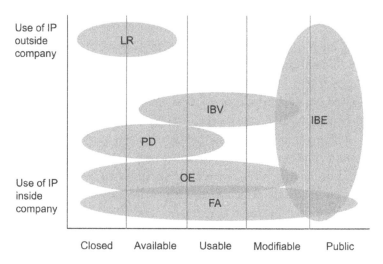

Fig. 7.4.   Sources of IP value with different degrees of openness and control over IP.

For Licensing Revenue (LR), the benefits result from use of closely controlled IP by other parties against an agreed compensation with the potential compensation or royalty level decreasing as the IP is more widely accessible. Likewise, to obtain Product Differentiation (PD) benefits, the IP is again usually tightly controlled, but in this case the user is the company itself, not an external entity. The differentiation potential of the IP diminishes as it becomes more openly available and easily utilizable. (However, it could be agreed that the IP is used by an external actor in another market.)

In contrast to these two, Freedom of Action (FA) benefits do not necessarily require that the IP would only be accessible or usable by the company itself. In many cases it may actually be in a company's best interest to try to commoditize the knowledge that the IP protects so that it will not be blocked out of its use. In some other cases, however, the company might see itself best protecting its freedom of action by keeping the IP as an unshared bargaining chip. In a similar fashion, Operational Efficiency benefits might be best utilized by sharing some parts of the IP with collaboration partners as well.

In order to benefit from IP through brand appreciation (IBV) or reputation, the company usually needs to be ready to collaborate and share parts of its know-how with other, known actors. Finally, in order to be able to get IBE benefits (influence in business environment) through steering, e.g. the technological development in the business environment in a favourable direction, the related IP needs to be accessible and utilizable by other, potentially completely unknown actors as well. In order for this to be successful, the IP needs to be taken into use by other companies as well.

Actions and Decisions Based on IP Strategy

An example of how different parts of IP strategy could be utilized in the enrichment of an idea of innovation or new business is presented in Fig. 7.5. IP and technology strategies should be able to assist in assigning the idea or invention to a technological area and assessing the importance of the technology to the company. Based on that, IP strategy could be used to determine the desired objective for IP in that technological area and the fit of the new idea in advancing that objective.

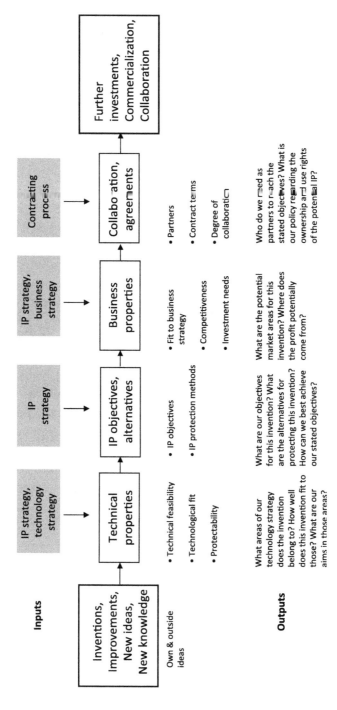

Fig. 7.5.   Using IP strategy in idea enrichment process.

Case example 7. Actions and decisions based on IP strategy

Two employees, one from Solar Power Systems Ltd and one from Vulcanus Control Systems Ltd, come up with a joint invention related to combining internet-based weather observation and forecast data with control systems of solar power production to match and optimize electricity production and consumption. Solar Power Systems need to decide how they will proceed with the invention together with Vulcanus Control Systems. They proceed to analyse the situation from the viewpoints described in Fig. 7.5.

Technical properties: In new installations, it is estimated that the invention (a new algorithm) could increase the efficiency of solar power production by 10 % in their main market areas. Additionally, Solar Power Systems think that the invention could be protected with a patent on its main market areas.

IP objectives: Solar Power Systems have established that their objectives for IT control systems (see Case example 6) are freedom of action (FA) and product differentiation (PD). Thus, they do not intend to license the technology out to other potential users. Currently, the IP portfolio of Solar Power Systems related to the technology is weak, and the technology needed is obtained from Vulcanus, who is a strong player in the field.

Business properties: Since the new invention could be easily installed on existing equipment, Solar Power Systems see that the market potential for the invention includes also the existing installed base of industrial solar power systems in addition to new customers. Additionally, the increased efficiency of the solar power production systems would work as a strong product differentiator.

Collaboration: Solar Power Systems conclude that, based on their IP strategy, it might be in both parties' interests if the resulting patent would be owned by Vulcanus Control Systems. It would be beneficial if Solar Power Systems would get a royalty-free licence for the invention and Vulcanus could, in turn, utilize the invention in other applications that are not competing with Solar Power Systems. Further development of the technology could also be more naturally done by Vulcanus, as the company has a higher level of knowledge on the area.

Questions Regarding Actions and Decisions on Transaction-type Networks

The questions in this and in the next section are for IP management related issues of networked innovation. They cover a broad range of aspects and they are partially overlapping with similar questions, criteria, and checklists related to collaboration and contracting (Chapters 5 and 10). There are different sets of questions for transaction and co-creation types of networked innovation due to the partially different nature of collaboration in these models. Questions related to transaction networks are given below, and questions related to co-creation networks in the next section.

Fit to current/future offerings (business strategy)

- What part of our offerings does the transferred IP relate to?
  - What are the potential market areas for this IP?
- What are our business objectives for this IP transaction?
- Where does the profit potentially come from?

Fit to current/future IP portfolio (technology strategy)

- What areas of our technology portfolio does the IP belong to?
  - Relevant technological or knowledge areas of the company
- What are our aims in those areas?
  - How does the knowledge increase our competitive advantage?
  - e.g. critical core knowledge or peripheral knowledge
- How well does this IP transaction fit to those?
  - When buying, are we sure that we get knowledge that is useful for us?
  - When selling, are we sure that we do not lose rights to critical knowledge?
- What protection tools are used or are going to be used in protecting the IP?
  - How is the transferred IP protected?
  - How does the protection fit our aims?

Questions to be considered together with network type selection

- What is our current and future position with respect to the seller/buyer of IP?
  - How dependent are we on the other party after the transaction?

Questions to be considered together with the contracting process

- What are the rights that are transferred?
  - o What kinds of rights are given to the buyer? What kinds of rights are retained by the seller?
  - o What kind of IP is involved (e.g. patents, copyrights)?
- What is the policy regarding ownership of transferred IP?
  - o How broad is the scope of transferred knowledge? How is it defined?
  - o Who has/who have the right to give further rights to third parties?
- What is the policy regarding use rights?
  - o Exclusive/non-exclusive licence
  - o Geographical scope of licensing
  - o Competitive/market scope

Questions Regarding Actions and Decisions on Co-creation-type Networks

Fit to current/future offerings (business strategy)

- What part of our offerings does the target of the co-creation relate to?
  - o Relevant business areas or business models that would utilize this knowledge
- How does the collaboration influence our offerings?
  - o Advantage that the new knowledge would bring about
- What are our business objectives in this collaboration?
- Where does the profit potentially come from?

Fit to current/future IP portfolio (technology strategy)

- What areas of our technology strategy does the collaboration relate to?
- What are our aims in those areas?
- How does the collaboration potentially influence our IP portfolio?
  - o Relevant technological or knowledge areas of the company
- How well does the objective of collaboration fit our aims?

Questions to be considered together with network type selection

- What are the roles and positions of the different parties of the collaboration?

- o Are we more dependent on the network partners as a result of the collaboration?
- What parts of our knowledge and IP is needed in the collaboration?
  - o How much resource and key personnel would need to be involved?

Questions to be considered together with the contracting process

- What is the policy regarding sharing of private information and degree of openness?
  - o Consideration of own core knowledge versus knowledge that can be shared with partners
  - o Trade-off between partner risk resulting from sharing critical private information and target risk of not sharing enough information to reach target
- What is the policy regarding ownership of potential resulting IP?
  - o How broad is the target of the collaboration? How is it defined?
  - o Who has/who have the right to give further rights to third parties?
- What is the policy regarding the scope of use rights of resulting IP?
  - o Exclusive/non-exclusive licence
  - o Geographical scope of licensing
  - o Competitive/market scope

Rights to Joint Work, Rewarding, and Profit Sharing

In networked innovation with several stakeholders, controlling IP becomes more complex. One recurring topic is the decision about who will own the rights to the results of joint work. This can be allocated in several alternative ways. Figure 7.6 describes the possible arrangements regarding the division of ownership of collaboration results between two companies. One of the companies can own all the results in the scope of collaboration, one of the companies can own its own work and joint work, or both companies own their own work and the joint work is owned together.

Joint ownership, where the companies jointly own the IP, may result in conflicting interests. For example, a product manufacturing company may use a patented technology for which the patent would be owned together with a pure R&D company. The R&D company might be eager to

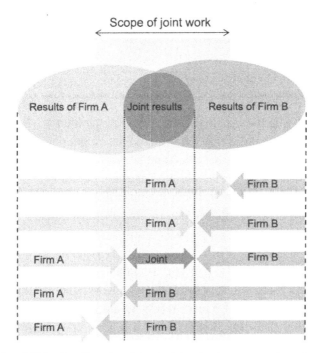

Fig. 7.6. Possibilities for allocating rights in joint development projects (modified from Gollin, 2008).

license the patented technology out to multiple companies to gain licensing revenue. However, the increased licensing revenue for both of the patent owners might not offset the increased competition that the manufacturing company would face in the markets and, accordingly, the diminished product differentiation value from the patent. Therefore, the manufacturing company would not be inclined to give any additional licences, leading to conflicting situations.

As the example suggests, allocation of the ownership of IP is not the only issue to be agreed. There are also other issues to be agreed on that may have a significant influence on the value of IP. According to Bader (2006), the most essential issues that need to be addressed regarding IPs in joint development are:

- Inventorship rights
- Ownership rights
- Rights of use

- Licensing rights
- Enforcement of rights
- Prosecution
- Administration of rights
- Sharing of costs

In a situation in which technologies are owned by a multitude of companies and the companies that develop the technologies might not commercialize them themselves, contracts have become increasingly important. In order to capture value from an IP, e.g. through licensing, the company needs to be able to agree with the licensee about the magnitude of the compensation, the nature of the licence (exclusive/non-exclusive) transfer of accompanying know-how and so forth.

From the perspective of IP valuation, the key issue for the success of a joint development project is that there is a definable value and motivation for collaboration for each of the parties. If the joint work is not profitable for all partners or the utility-sharing mechanisms in the collaboration encourage free-riding rather than true commitment, a lack of commitment towards collaboration tends to follow and otherwise profitable and marketable technologies are either not developed or commercialized (see e.g. Hytönen and Jarimo, 2008).

A simplified example for illustrating different roles and compensations in collaboration with three companies is depicted in Fig. 7.7. In the figure, agreements are made with respect to ownership of the resulting IP (arrows with solid line), use rights or licences to the resulting IP (arrows with dashed line) and direct or indirect (from future profits) monetary compensation (arrows with dotted line). In the example, company 2 acts as a research subcontractor for company 1, giving the resulting IP to company 1 in exchange for monetary compensation. Company 3, which does not take part in the R&D work, gets a use right to the results from the final owner of the work. If the potential profits to partners and the risks related to those can be estimated with a reasonable accuracy, it would be valuable to analyse through simulations whether a commitment to collaboration is in all partners' interests. The system dynamic approach (see e.g. Sterman, 2000) or game theory, for example, can be used to analyse the commitment.

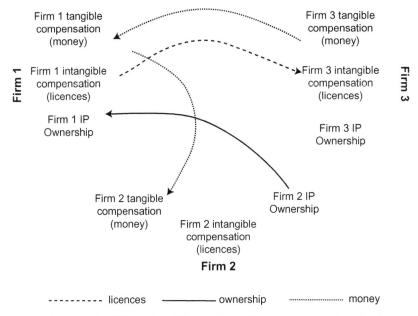

Fig. 7.7. An example of illustrating different roles and compensations in joint development.

In these kinds of joint development projects, short-term monetary gains and the final payback from the project are often contradictory objectives. In joint development projects involving complex technologies, tacit and specialized knowledge, or end results that are partly indefinable in advance, it is difficult to assess just how much effort has been put into getting the obtained results and whether the results could have been significantly improved with marginal additional contributions. This emphasizes the importance of agreeing about such win–win incentives and rewards in the collaboration that best possible end results are in every partner's interests.

Part IV

PRACTICES AND ACTIONS

Networked Business
- Description of collaboration models
- Guide for collaboration

IP Strategy
- Description of IP strategy
- Guide for collaboration

Practices & Actions
- Methods of knowledge protection
- Contracting process
- Contractual check-lists
- Glossary

Chapter 8

Methods of Knowledge Protection

The ways of protecting knowledge can, in general, be divided into three categories according to their formality: formal protection methods often called intellectual property rights (IPR), contractual (semi-formal) protection methods, and informal protection methods (PRO INNO Europe, 2007). Formal protection methods arise from IP legislation and include patents, trademarks, utility models, rights to commercial names, and copyrights. Contractual/semi-formal protection methods include different types of contracts, such as confidentiality agreements, prohibition of competition clauses in agreements, and proprietary and access rights clauses in agreements. Brief descriptions of the formal and contractual methods of knowledge protection are given in the Glossary in this book. An easy access to the intellectual property laws is AIPPI, which is a non-government organization for the law relating to the protection of intellectual property.

Informal protection methods attempt to prevent the loss of key knowledge or restrict undesirable access to sensitive information either inside the firm or in external relations. Secrecy is one of the main methods of informal knowledge protection. Secrecy means that key knowledge is kept secret either from some of the employees inside the company or from external co-operation partners such as customers and business partners. Publishing can also be used as a method of knowledge protection: it prevents others from appropriating the knowledge, thus confirming the freedom of action for the firm. Publishing can also be used to prevent other companies from claiming patents in the same area. Access to sensitive key information inside the business may be restricted to a certain limited group of people preventing the loss of key knowledge to unwanted parties. It may mean, for example, that certain employees or external actors are not allowed to

Table 8.1.   Common methods for the protection of knowledge.

Formal protection methods	Contractual protection methods	Informal protection methods
— Patent	— Non-competition	— Secrecy
— Utility model	— Confidentiality	— Publishing
— Trademark	— Recruitment freeze	— Restricted access to information
— Design right	— Employee invention	— Confidentiality
— Copyright	— Proprietary and access rights	— Client relationship management
		Loyalty building among personnel
		— Circulation of staff between tasks
		— Division of duties or subcontracting
		— Distributed product design
		— Fast innovation rhythm
		— Complex design/technical protection

access particular files or databases. Confidentiality as an informal protection method for knowledge implies confidential relationships between reliable partners without formal contracts. Effective client relationship management tends to prevent knowledge leakage when the client relationship ends and is particularly important in service business where service innovations are co-created with customers. Trust building is important for maintaining the personnel loyalty to the employer. Effective strategies, such as financial incentives, training opportunities, or good career prospects are suitable for keeping the personnel loyal to the company. Circulating staff between tasks can be used as a means to decrease the dependence on individual employees. Division of duties or subcontracting imply that work tasks within the business are divided into fractions between employees and actors, which prevents the leakage of the overall concept of a new service or product. Distributed product design means that the design process is divided into fractions so that individual designers know only a fraction of the process, which prevents possible leakage of the product design to outsiders. Fast innovation rhythm is a frequently used means to protect business and to keep the company one step ahead of the competitors. Complex design makes it difficult or even impossible for an employee, customer, or partner to imagine the concrete structure of the product. Technical protection contains different kinds of instruments to protect IP, for example software encryption, security keys, and code obfuscation. Informal protection practices also help capture tacit knowledge and transform it into explicit knowledge, which can then be shared within the company. That will decrease a company's risks and dependence on individual employees (PRO INNO Europe, 2007; Päällysaho and Kuusisto, 2008).

An overview of typical methods for knowledge protection in business is given in Table 8.1 (modified from WIPO; PRO INNO Europe, 2007). Note that the set is not complete but the emphasis of the table is on the methods that have an importance when opening innovation.

Chapter 9

The Contracting Process

In this chapter the guidelines for managing the contracting process are presented. In innovation networks contracting needs to be seen as a process beginning from preparations and negotiations continuing to the post-contractual phase. The actual contract check-lists are given in Chapter 10. Chapters 9 and 10 are intended to be used in conjunction with the guide for networked business in Chapter 5 and the guide for IP strategy in Chapter 7. Questions and issues presented in those chapters should be clear and understood before designing the actual contract contents.

Guidelines for Contracting

The contracts of networked innovation involving intellectual property issues can range from simple contracts made between two parties to complex contracts with multiple parties and multiple commitments between companies in a network. Bader (2006) describes the different collaborative settings as bilateral, or one-to-one, multilateral, or one-to-many, and collateral, or many-to-many. These are illustrated in Fig. 9.1.

The particular business model and the collaboration model set their own requirements for contracting. In these different settings the functions of a contract document are also different to a certain extent. Understanding the important functions of the contract in question makes it easier to manage the whole contracting process. These functions can be divided into two categories: framework functions and practical functions (Table 9.1) (Nystén-Haarala, 2008). The framework functions concern value creation and commitment and can be seen as some kind of core objectives for a contractual relation. The practical functions such as co-ordinating,

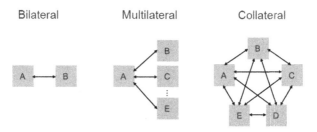

Fig. 9.1.   Different collaborative settings of R&D collaborations.

Table 9.1.   Functions of contracts in innovation networks (modified from Nyotén Haarala, 2000).

Framework Functions	Practical Functions
• Value creation • Commitment	• Co-ordinating • Safeguarding • Contingency adaptability and dispute settlement

safeguarding, contingency planning, and dispute settlement are more connected with concrete clauses in contract contents and in concrete contract management.

Contracts are often only seen as legal documents for protecting against risks. They can, however, also work as tools for organizing collaboration and introducing flexibility into the network. A contract document itself can be seen as an instrument for managing the network and formalizing the innovation process. Emphasis of different functions varies according to the collaboration model. This may mean for example that as collaboration in the network increases, contract terms on co-ordinating and dealing with contingencies will increase compared to terms dealing with safeguarding the contracting parties against risks (Eckhard and Mellewigt, 2006). However, contractual clauses can seldom be interpreted to execute one particular function, but usually different clauses have many functions and vice versa. In the R&D collaboration setting, the most important issues in contracts are sharing of rights and benefits and, on the other hand, the responsibilities and costs from the collaboration between collaborating partners.

Framework functions

Framework functions, which are value creation and commitment, are connected with each other and are both crucial functions of business, providing the framework for contracting. In general, business contracts are made to create or capture value, meaning that business goals define the framework of contracting. Value creation should be a precondition for business contracting, since without creating value, at least in the long run, there is usually no real need for the collaboration or the contract. However, value creation is a difficult function to separate from other functions of contract, because the entire contract and business itself functions to create value (Nystén-Haarala, 2008). The other framework element of a contract is commitment. Contracts bring forth obligations and responsibilities, which contracting parties themselves can define.

These two functions and aims can be detected in contract contents but in addition they also work as framework conditions. In this way, the *limitation of competition* creates value, for example, but on the other hand protects the leakage of knowledge and binds for the shared goal (Haapio and Haavisto, 2005). If the interdependence between the parties is firm, parties can accept some amount of faults during the contractual relation and handle better the occasional dissatisfaction. Anyhow, the real enthusiasm for the collaboration and commitment arises from different motives than the need to write a contract document.

Practical functions

Classification of the *practical functions* is not an easy task, as one contract clause may contain several elements of contractual functions. Contracts can be seen as tools for risk management, as according to Williamson (1985) the function and meaning of a contract is to protect oneself against the possible opportunistic behaviour of the other contracting party. Risk management is not therefore considered to be a separate function, but the whole contract and all the functions on some level are considered to be part of risk management. *Safeguarding functions* can be seen to be at the core of risk management.

By *co-ordination function* we mean that a contractual relationship should be co-ordinated also with actual contractual clauses. Co-ordination includes, for example, terms of division of the roles and responsibilities, contract management, control and communication and project management with timetable, reporting, etc. In our opinion, a clear and well-organized collaboration and reaching the shared goal must be supported with good terms of co-ordination.

Contract terms considering clauses of *contingency management* are adapted to contracts in order to reduce the risk of ending up in a situation where an unproductive and unprofitable contract has to be performed. Contingency management tools have to be provided for changes in both internal and external circumstances of the contractual relationship. There is also a positive demand for it: contingency planning needs to be done for possibilities, not only for threats. In the case of disagreements, dispute settlement in innovation networks is recommended as being arranged through private ordering, either between the parties (bilateral ordering) or through trilateral ordering, such as mediator or arbitrator proceedings, for flexibility, quickness, and maintaining the secrecy.

IP management may be considered as one of the core issues in innovation network contracts, but it is clear that IP management is important in all contract functions, and cannot be considered as a totally distinct contractual area. However, in the check-lists of this workbook IP management is treated separately in order to keep things accessible and for ease of implementing IP management into contracts. The means of contractual IP management depends on the content of collaboration and the shared goal, meaning that IP can be managed for example by licence terms and confidentiality, but also through co-ordination and communication clauses, when co-ordination function is linked with the management of the collaboration and the whole project. This includes assignment of roles, allocation of control and communication, timetable, reporting, etc., which all are fundamental issues in IP management.

Consequently, the contracting process and the content of the contract document itself should take into account the type of innovation network as well as the actors in the network. In some collaboration models, especially in transaction networks, the safeguarding risk management aspect is highlighted; while in co-creation networks flexible co-ordination aspects may be more important. Contracts play different roles in different phases of the innovation process. R&D contracts and collaboration contracts have different aims than contracts in the commercialization phase. Due to this, emphasis of different contractual functions and capabilities has to be taken into consideration. Since contracts are a means of private ordering, the level and definitions of commitment are connected with the motivations and business purposes of the parties. In the following, the important contractual functions in both co-creation and transaction networks are presented.

Contractual functions in co-creation networks

Co-creation networks are characterized by nested and interconnected relationships. In these networks there are heterogeneous actors with varying interests and roles. There may be explicit background IP at the core of the co-creation initiation, but tacit knowledge, however, plays a highly important role. The framework functions, meaning value creation and the commitment of the parties into collaboration are highlighted in these contracts. The collaboration is greatly based on shared interests and trust between partners and when the common goal is no longer shared, there may not be further potential for collaboration anymore.

Nevertheless, regardless of trust between the partners, a formal contract protecting the rights and obligations of the parties, and extending the root of the collaboration from the initial personal relationships to a formal company level, should exist. To find the right balance between trust and the contract contents in the early stage of the exploration phase, companies should conclude a brief but adequate frame agreement where they agree on the intentions of the collaboration, on the main points of the development project, and on the main points related to the exploitation of the potential innovation outcome. Contracts can also be supported by informal rules of the game or more specified rules of a community. One needs to bear in mind that the formal support of legal (public) governance gets less defined the more open the collaboration gets.

Contracts in co-creation networks require dynamics (agility) in changed circumstances and dynamic co-ordination aspects should play an important role in the contracts. Definition of the purposes and commitment to collaboration are the key elements of co-creation contracts. Efficient and proper contingency and change management interpreting the shared goal is also highly important.

Contractual functions in transaction networks

Contracts in transaction networks can be approached from defining obligations and rights of the parties and can be set in a more detailed manner. Closed contracts used in transaction networks, such as licence agreements, are often bilateral and relationships and interaction in general are simple. The transferred knowledge is mainly explicit with clear formal protection. The IP is managed and protected by formal contracts where a risk management aspect plays an important role. Therefore, all practical functions, such as co-ordinating, safeguarding, and contingency management are considered to be important and, in general, they are easily managed in contracts like licence agreements and the sale of goods.

Negotiations

The negotiation phase before signing the contract can be considered as very important as it defines the frames for the collaboration and therefore also the main issues of the contract contents. Negotiations are a part of the contracting process, e.g. the management of contracts from the initiation phase through negotiations and design until implementation and well-managed termination of contracts.

The tools for preparing for negotiations are presented in this section. Contract design and negotiation phases are partly overlapping, and thus should be considered and managed at the same time. Often collaboration already occurs during the negotiations and design phases of contract.

Preparing well and at the same time being aware of the firm's strategic decisions also seems to have an effective impact on the result of the negotiations. The negotiator's confidence in his arguments and awareness of his goals strengthens his negotiating power, meaning that the negotiator must know what he wants to achieve before negotiations begin. Time limitations often make negotiations challenging. Before entering into negotiations, the questions presented in Table 9.2 should be answered. Important guidelines for preparing for negotiations are presented in previous parts of the workbook. They should be read through before using the following tools.

Negotiations and drafting the contracts are partly overlapping phases of the contracting process. Please find below aspects to be considered before drafting the contract (Wright and Fergusson, 2009):

- Be aware of a company's strategies
- Use your internal check-lists, guidelines, and procedures

Table 9.2. Guidelines for preparing for negotiations.

What are our strategies? **What is our negotiation strategy?**	• Business strategy, IP strategy, and contract strategy • Business benefits of particular collaboration • Preparing for negotiations is team work between different departments of the organization: law, sales, engineering, project management etc. • Guidelines and check-lists as support
How are the risks analysed?	• Evaluation of risks • Risk planning
What is the importance of this particular contract?	• Our goals and interests in the partnership or network • The prospective duration of the partnership/network
What is the shared goal of the parties?	• The shared goal (or the idea of it) of the parties • Planning the shared goal and strategy in collaboration • Partnership thinking and the principle of reciprocity
What is the validity of negotiations?	• Confidentiality • Memorandum of understanding, preliminary agreements • Pre-contractual liability • Sanctions for infringing the Confidentiality agreement (NDA) and other obligations concerning the negotiations
Is there also collaboration with others? **Is there something special about this particular collaboration?**	• Confidentiality agreement • Restraint of competition • Effects on the negotiations with others

(Continued)

Table 9.2. (*Continued*)

Should we protect the new ideas already at this stage? If yes, in which way?	• Confidentiality agreement
	• Network capabilities and trust building
	• Guidelines for communication
How do we decide to continue?	• Continue into collaboration
	• Put the process on hold
	• Turn it back to idea enrichment or opportunity analysis
	• Stop the process

- Focus on outcomes rather than boundaries
- Allow flexibility in selecting terms and risks
- Create well-defined contract procedures
- Clearly allocate roles and responsibilities
- Establish an execution environment that is proactive and forward thinking
- Design a co-operative form of contract encouraging collaboration
- Always make a written agreement, also preliminary agreements in a written form
- Be aware of both mandatory and non-mandatory legislation and ascertain if there is need or possibilities to agree differently
- Be open minded
- Communicate internally within the company

Implementation

Contractual responsibilities and collaboration are performed in the implementation phase. Contracts need to be designed proactively so that flexibility and opportunities to modify and develop the agreement (evolving contract) are available in the implementation phase. The implementation of the contract also requires continuous inter-firm collaboration such as sharing the roles and tasks, communication, and follow-up. Consider the following aspects when implementing the contract:

- Internal distribution of contract information
- Activate the persons in charge

- Share the tasks and contractual obligations
- Execute the co-operation of contract team and project team
- Make clear the impacts of contract
- Manage openness of input, process, and output (results)
- Follow up the implementation
- Report and communicate
- Sustain and strengthen the partnership

Termination and the Post-contractual Phase

Contracts can come to an end for different reasons. Depending on the reasons, whether insurmountable problems occurred or the contract period simply came to an end, termination of the contractual relation requires some strategic decisions and actions. The following questions in Table 9.3

Table 9.3. Guidelines for termination of the contract and post-contractual phase.

What are the rules and guidelines for termination?	• Agreements
	• Guidelines for monitoring IP activities
	• Guidelines for evaluating IP
	• Guidelines for innovation intention
	• Mandatory rules of attribution and accessibility in law
Do we have the competence to continue or repeat?	**Can we continue**? (Collaboration or other innovation practices)
	— Motivation and competence
	— Contract terms: access, non-complete, re-negotiations
	— Accessibility provided by law
	— Evaluation of collaboration (targets, performance, sharing the risks and benefits)
	Should we continue?
	— Strategic consideration
	— Are we willing to pay for the continued accessibility?

(Continued)

Table 9.3.   (*Continued*)

Do we have the competence to change?	**Change management**
	— Administrative change
	— Contract modification
	— Constructive change
	— Acceleration of performance
	— Budgetary changes
	— Re-negotiations and re-signing
Do we have the competence to terminate?	**Termination causes**
	— Completing the performance
	— Annulment
	— Impossibility to perform
	— Erroneous interpretation of contract
	— Failure to co-operate
	— Improperly exercized options
	— Termination of a particular term
	— Completing of injunctions
	— Breach of contract, infringements
	Disputes and surviving claims
	— NDA
	— Warranties
	— Indemnification
How to manage IPRs at this point?	**Re-examination of your own and your partner's IPRs**
	— Still valid IPR, cost/benefit
	— Who has and who is using the critical knowledge/IPR
	— Us alone
	— Current partners
	— New partners
	— Third parties

(*Continued*)

Table 9.3.   (*Continued*)

	— Possibility to negotiate
	— Maintenance of right (IPR valuation)
	— Maintain tacit knowledge or not
	— Decisions for the information accumulated
	— Continued sharing/division
	— Shared/joint ownership — Separate agreement
In case of termination of the contract what are the decisions connected to the business model and the company's strategies?	• IPR and IP management, managing the know-how-based knowledge • Stopping or not using the received knowledge • IPR enforcement strategy • Maintaining the IPR or not • Maintaining tacit knowledge or not • Competition and infringement monitoring
If part of contractual terms stay valid after termination, what to do with them?	• Confidentiality • IPR • Continuing with different contract, implementation of new terms

are presented to guide in situations where the contractual collaboration is about to come to an end. In these situations the causes of termination have to be defined and analysed before making the decision whether to continue or terminate the contract. If the conclusion is termination of the contract, there are issues that need to be considered before the termination; the IP strategy of the firm also has to cover this phase. Intellectual property rights and other important knowledge resulting from collaboration continue to be managed and protected even when the contract ends. In this phase the issues considering the post-contractual phase also have to be decided. Before the termination of a contract, the highlighted questions should be answered.

Chapter 10

Contractual Check-lists

In this chapter we present check-lists for contract contents. The primary task of the check-lists is to remind users of important legal and commercial issues that should be taken into account when designing contracts for open and networked innovation and business. The check-lists are not exhaustive and they have to be modified and adjusted according to the firm's strategies and decisions. Before using the following check-lists and guidelines, it is recommended that the workbook is read through from the beginning and that the guidelines presented in the earlier chapters are followed.

Firstly, there are check-lists for preliminary agreement and guidelines for confidentiality issues, which should be considered in both transaction and co-creation networks. Secondly, there are check-lists specific to co-creation and transaction networks. Check-lists for co-creation networks include guidelines for open source and collaboration agreements. Check-lists for transaction networks include supply agreements, licence agreements, and consultant agreements. However, the division of check-lists according to network models is not strict and with appropriate and specific modifications and combinations these can be used in both models. For example, there may well be a need for a consultant agreement in a co-creation network, and the check-list for consultant agreements in the section "Agreements for Transaction Networks" in this chapter, although positioned among the check-lists for transaction networks, gives good advice for the design of a consultant contract.

A list of the presented check-lists is given in Table 10.1. The structure and content of the contractual check-lists is presented in Table 10.2. Explanations for the terms used in the check-lists are given in the Glossary.

Table 10.1.   List of contractual check-lists.

Agreements common to co-creation and transaction networks	• Non-disclosure agreement • Letter of intent • Preliminary agreement
Agreements for co-creation networks	• Collaboration agreement • Guidelines for licensing open source software
Agreements for transaction networks	• Licence agreement • Software licence agreement I Consultant agreement • Supply agreement

Table 10.2.   Structure and content of contractual check-lists.

Notices	• Interpretation material for particular contract
Regulation	• Both non-mandatory and possible mandatory rules related to particular agreement • Mandatory rules include certain rights of employee in employment law, competition law, and tax law • List is not exhaustive
Frame	• Content of particular agreement in general • Specifications are in boxes below
Co-ordination	• Terms considered in project management • Roles and responsibilities of parties
IP management	• Terms considering IPR and IP management • Confidentiality (see also check-list for NDA)
Safeguarding	• Risk management • Terms considering the liabilities and indemnification of parties • Warranties and how to deal with them
Contingency management	• Alternatives for management of contingencies • Internal and external changes • Flexibility and dynamics in contracts
Dispute settlement	• Alternatives for procedures of dispute settlement • Applied law

Agreements Common to Co-creation and Transaction Networks

A non-disclosure agreement (NDA) is often signed when entering into negotiations. A NDA sets up a framework where the parties can open their knowledge to each other from the beginning. For the interim intentions of collaboration, a letter of intent (LOI) or a memorandum of understanding (MOU) may be written during the negotiations. There may also be a preliminary agreement which obligates the parties to further contracts. When details concerning the collaboration become apparent, the main contract can be assigned.

Confidentiality and non-disclosure agreement

NDAs can be agreed between business partners, but also between an employee and an employer. They are utilized for ensuring the confidentiality of ideas, business secrets, and other confidential material. The first confidentiality document is usually signed at the beginning of negotiations and can be considered to support the openness between actors. Before drafting the confidentiality or other agreements, the following questions presented in Table 10.3 should be answered. In Table 10.4, there is the check-list for drafting a NDA.

Letter of intent (LOI)

A letter of intent differs from a preliminary agreement in its ability to bind the parties legally. An LOI is not necessarily an obligation to further agreements (see Table 10.5). The possibility of pre-contractual liability should, however, be considered. An LOI can be, but does not have to be, detailed. When making further agreements, the LOI is usually overruled, but drafting of it still requires care. When drafting the letter of intent, the issues mentioned in the "Frame" column in the table may be considered in desired specificity. The most important issues are in bold.

Preliminary agreement

Preliminary agreement obliges parties to conclude a (main) contract and to ensure that its validity is the same as further contracts. A preliminary agreement can be done when all important issues related to the contract or collaboration are not clear at the beginning of the collaboration. A check-list for the preliminary agreement is presented in Table 10.6. In co-creation

Table 10.3.   Guidelines for the confidentiality in the collaboration.

How do we define the IP in our company? **How do we define the confidential information? What is included in it and what is left outside?**	• For example: "IP includes not only IP rights that are granted and protected by the laws, but also the knowledge and other intangible resources whose use may be controlled by contracts, policies, organization and process routines and norms, both physically and technically" (Chapter 1).
What is our strategy for confidential IP and other information?	• Management of the transfer of confidential IP and information • The uncertainty of NDA • Risk analysis of what could happen if the confidential IP or information spreads • Balance between managing and minimizing the risks and collaboration in open atmosphere
What are our interests for the IP or other information kept confidential?	• Intention to patent • Strategically important IP or information
What are the restrictions and limitations and how limited we can be?	• Openness concerning the IP which is not so important • Reciprocity
What is the procedure in case some confidential information has to be transferred or otherwise we want to make an exception of the NDA?	• Defining the reasons, for example new supplier, subcontractor, or employee who is participating • Re-negotiations • Change to contract or oral agreement
With whom do we do the NDAs in our company? What are the roles of parties in contracts?	• Business partners • Employee • Subcontractor/supplier and their employees
How far do we chain the NDAs?	• Subcontractors/suppliers • Interest groups of subcontractors/suppliers • Employees of subcontractors/suppliers also with individual responsibility
When do we want to use NDA?	• Pre-non-disclosure • Post-non-disclosure
Is the NDA incoming, outgoing, or two-way?	• Interests of the drafter • Confidentiality of network (common or separate)

(Continued)

Table 10.3. (*Continued*)

What other agreements are there?	• Collaboration agreement • Licence agreement • Other agreements
How long will the NDA be in force?	• Continuing confidentiality after termination of other agreements • Patenting
When do we establish separate NDAs, when the NDA is included into (part of) the main contract?	• Considering the emphasis of confidential IP and information • Bilateral or multilateral NDA • The content of other agreements
How are the disagreements solved?	• Litigation • Bilateral governance: negotiations • Third party governance: arbitration, mediator • Applied law
How can we ensure the permanence of the NDA?	• **In contract contents**: clauses and terms, legislation, other sources of interpretation • **In contractual process**: control, co-ordination, communication, IP management • **In relational level**: communication, trust, management of openness • Do we have other arguments, such as trade secret?

Table 10.4. Check-list for non-disclosure agreement (NDA).

Notices	• NDA • Other related and previous agreements
Regulation	• No special enactment • CISG • General contractual principles • Commercial law • Copyright law • Patent law • Employment law
NDA Frame	1. Parties 2. Object of contract and introduction 3. Definitions of special terms used in contract 4. Shared goal 5. Confidentiality 6. Roles and responsibilities

(*Continued*)

Table 10.4.   (*Continued*)

	7. Terms of confidentiality
	8. Terms of termination of contract
	9. Liquidated damages
	10. Changes to contract
	11. Transfer of contract
	12. Applied law
	13. Dispute resolution
Object of Non-disclosure	• Definition of IP and other confidential information • Definitions of what is not considered to be confidential • Parties right to use the above defined information and limitations to it • Conditions under which this information can be disclosed and to whom (usually agreement includes specific terms for this and changes have to be agreed formally). • Often the confidentiality continues after termination of the main contract and collaboration
Safeguarding	• **Breach of contract** — Liabilities and limitations — Liquidated damages — Direct damages — Consequential damages • **Other businesses and how the confidentiality effects on them** • *Force majeure* • **Transfer of contract** • **Choosing the best procedure for resolution of disagreements and infringements** — Litigation — Bilateral governance: negotiations — Third party governance: arbitration, mediator • **Liquidated damages** • **Applied law**

Table 10.5.   Check-list for Letter of intent (LOI).

Notices	• Letter of intent • Related and previous agreements • NDA
Regulation	• No special enactment • CISG (non-mandatory sale of goods regulation) • Commercial law • Copyright law

(*Continued*)

Table 10.5. (*Continued*)

	•	Patent law
	•	Employment law
	•	Competition law
LETTER OF INTENT	1.	Parties of LOI
Frame	2.	Introduction and object of LOI
	3.	Definitions of special terms used in LOI
	4.	**Shared goal**
	5.	Negotiation schedule and process
	6.	Possible further agreements
	7.	**Confidentiality**
	8.	Roles and responsibilities
	9.	IP management
	10.	Prohibition of competition?
	11.	Defray of costs
	12.	Term of LOI
	13.	Terms of termination of LOI
	14.	**Pre-contractual liability**?
	15.	Possible infringements and penalty and applied law

Table 10.6. Check-list for preliminary agreements.

Notices	•	Preliminary agreement
	•	Other related or previous agreements
		— NDA
		— Letter of intent
Regulation	•	No special enactment
	•	CISG
	•	General contractual principles
	•	Commercial law
	•	Copyright law
	•	Patent law
	•	Employment law
PRELIMINARY AGREEMENT	1.	Parties
Frame	2.	Introduction and background of collaboration
	3.	Definitions of special terms used in agreements
	4.	**Shared goal**
	5.	Further agreements
	6.	Further negotiation schedule and process
	7.	**Roles and responsibilities of parties**
	8.	**IP management**
	9.	**Pre-contractual liability**

(*Continued*)

Table 10.6. (*Continued*)

	10. **Confidentiality**
	11. In case conditions cannot be fulfilled, what are the consequences
	12. Prohibition of competition
	13. **Defray of costs**
	14. Term of agreement
	15. Terms of termination
	16. Infringements and penalty
	17. **Applied law**
Co-ordination	• **Roles and responsibilities**
	Roles and responsibilities of parties
	— Mechanisms for developing and follow-up the collaboration
	• **Contract management**
	— Project organization, who, how, when
	— Reporting risks, evaluation, analysing, quality
	— Communication
	— Negotiation schedule and timeframe
	— Price
	— Costs
IP management	• **Definition of IP**
	• **Sharing documentation and information**
	• **Confidentiality**
	— If the intention is to patent, this has to be noticed in confidentiality clause and agreement
	— Separate NDA
	• **Definitions and rights for background and results**
	— Rights to the background, usually background has to be listed in agreement or appendices
	— Ownership and exploitation of results
	• Proprietary rights (patent right, copyright, trademark, etc.)
	• Right to use the results of development (licences, see Licence agreement)
	• Exclusive or non-exclusive right to market and sell

networks, the preliminary agreement could be considered as the first step towards binding collaboration. Preliminary agreement can be, but does not have to be, detailed. However, when drafting care should be taken for the issues mentioned in the "Frame" column in the table. The most important issues are in bold.

Agreements for co-creation networks

Collaboration agreement

Collaboration agreement can mean any agreement where two or more companies are working towards a shared goal. A network can consist of a wide variety of actors, for example subcontractors, suppliers, and a system integrator, and the shared goal can vary. Depending on a company's interest and role, the emphasis of contractual elements and terms is different. The most critical issues in collaboration agreements are agreeing on the shared goal, responsibilities of parties, sharing of IP, rights to background information and outcome, and the sharing of profits and costs. Main issues and procedural rules have to be agreed clearly, but specifications can be complemented later. A check-list for the collaboration agreement is in Table 10.7.

Table 10.7.   Check-list for collaboration agreements.

Notices	• Collaboration agreement • Rules concerning public funding • NDA • Other related and previous agreements • Standard contracts, general conditions • Sales terms
Regulation	• No special enactment • CISG • General contractual principles • Commercial law • Copyright law • Patent law • Tax law • Employment law • Competition law
COLLABORATION AGREEMENT **Frame**	1. Parties 2. Object of contract and introduction to the collaboration 3. Definitions of special terms used in contract 4. Shared goal 5. Roles and responsibilities 6. Contract management 7. IP management 8. Safeguarding

(Continued)

Table 10.7.   (*Continued*)

	9. Contingency management
	10. Dispute settlement
	11. Term of contract (duration)
	12. Terms of termination of contract
	13. Applied law
Co-ordination	• **Roles and responsibilities**
	— Roles and responsibilities of parties
	— Roles and responsibilities of possible co-ordinator
	— Mechanisms for developing and follow-up the collaboration
	— Rights to use other subcontractors
	• **Contract management**
	— Project organization
	— Communication
	— Decisions, approvals, defaults
	— Documentation
	— Reporting risks, evaluation, quality measurements
	— Follow-up
	— Schedule
	— Price
	— Terms of payment
	— Costs
	— Taxation
	— Sales terms
	— Approval of the results
	— Invoicing
	— Post assessments
IP management	• **Definition of IP**
	• **If background or part of it is protected by a patent or registered design, then usually:**
	— The party warrants it owns the IP and that it does not infringe third party's rights
	— The party must maintain the IPR during the contract
	— The party may be obliged to act against an infringer of the IP
	• **Confidentiality**
	— The potential intention to patent has to be noticed in confidentiality clause and agreement
	• **Considering the need for following**
	— Recruitment freeze
	— Prohibition of competition
	— Separate NDA

(*Continued*)

Table 10.7. (*Continued*)

	• **Definitions and rights to background and results** — Rights to the background, usually background has to be listed in agreement or appendices — Ownership and exploitation of results • Proprietary rights (patent right, copyright, trademark, etc.) • Right to use the results of development (licences, see Licence agreement) • Exclusive or non-exclusive right to market and sell
Safeguarding	• **Warranties** — The parties may be required to warrant that the quality of their work and contribution conform to the agreement • **Liabilities and limitations** — If the parties intend to limit their liability for a defective performance, this should be stated — Terms of liabilities for direct damages and consequential damages — Terms of time when risk of loss or damage to the goods passes from one party to another — Terms of time when the ownership passes from one party to another • **Transfer of contract** • **Other businesses** • *Force majeure* • **Applied law**
Contingency management	• **Re-negotiations** • **Index clause** • **Transfer of contract** • *Force majeure*
Dispute settlement	• **Choosing the best procedure for resolution of disagreements, management of performance problems, and infringements** — Bilateral governance: negotiations — Third party governance: arbitration, mediator • **Liquidated damages** • **Applied law**

Open source

Open source by definition means free access to the software in a source code form. Open source also offers the free right to distribute the software and the code, also as a part of combined software. Open source code is free for users to make modifications, improve the code, and create derivative works. Normally the results of improvements and changes have to be shared with other users in the community, meaning that the distribution has to be permitted both as source code and as reversed form. In these cases royalties and other payments are prohibited (Open Source Initiative; Välimäki, 2009). The open source definition (OSD) is approved by the open source initiative (OSI) for the licences which fulfil the terms of OSD. When passing the acceptance procedure of OSI the licence may have the "open source" certification. More detailed information about open source is given on the OSI website. The most common open source licences are listed below in Table 10.8. Before making decisions about using open source in business, careful consideration and exploration of the field is recommended in order to manage the risks better and using the benefits of open source in a right way (Välimäki, 2009). To look for more information about the licences, see the OSI website.

Before licensing open source software, the following issues should also be considered in addition to the other check-lists and guidelines of this workbook:

- Development and open source policy and procedures, considering the business strategy, IP-strategy, and contracting strategy
- Decide and define the proper role of open source software in business and strategy
- The benefit of team work between different departments of the organization, such as management, engineering, and legal counsel
- Take advantage of the commercial tools and services

Table 10.8.   Categorization of the most common open source licences.

Permissive licences	Non-permissive copyleft (GNU) licences	Permanent licences, share alike
— Permits redistributors to combine the licensed code to other software and adding restrictions to derived work — MIT, BSD, Apache	— GNU GPL, GNU LGPL, Mozilla Public Licence — Non-permissive licences become binding when copy is distributed forward — The derived work has to be licensed back with bsame terms as a separate component	— Does not set obligation to license the combination, but permits linking the components as-part of a combination

- Consider the quality of open source (OSI)
- Prefer standards
- Make clear what rights, obligations, and restrictions certain open source licence includes
- Create an efficient risk management plan for

  - The uncertainty of using the licence correctly
  - Infringement of a third party's rights
  - Risks of combining proprietary software with open source software
  - Internal and external changes and disagreements

Agreements for Transaction Networks

Licence agreement

Licence agreement is an agreement authorizing the licensee to the property of licensor under the incorporeal rights (see Table 10.9). It is a provision

Table 10.9. Check-list for licence agreements.

Notices	• Licence agreement • Sales terms • Other related and previous agreements — NDA — Service agreement — Collaboration agreement • Standard contract (general conditions)
Regulation	• No special enactment • General contractual principles • Commercial law • Copyright law • Patent law • Tax law • Product liability • Employment law • Competition law
LICENCE AGREEMENT **Frame**	1. Parties 2. Object of agreement and introduction 3. Definitions of special terms used in contract 4. Licence management 5. Possible co-development 6. Possible related services 7. Contract management

(Continued)

Table 10.9.   (*Continued*)

<table>
<tr><td></td><td colspan="2">8. IP management
9. Safeguarding
10. Contingency management
11. Dispute settlement
12. Term of contract
13. Terms of termination of contract
14. Applied law</td></tr>
<tr><td>**Co-ordination**</td><td>•</td><td>**Contract management**
— Project organization
— Timetable
— Price
— Terms of payment
— Reporting
— Sales terms
— Follow-up</td></tr>
<tr><td></td><td>•</td><td>**Possible co-development (see collaboration agreement)**
— Shared goal
— Roles and responsibilities of Licensor and Licensee
— Mechanisms for developing and follow-up the collaboration
— Rights to use other subcontractors</td></tr>
<tr><td></td><td>•</td><td>**Possible related services**</td></tr>
<tr><td>**Licence
management**</td><td>•
•</td><td>**Definition of IP**
**If the licensed product or service is protected by a
patent or registered design, then usually;**
— The Licensor warrants that it owns the IPR which does not infringe third party rights
— The Licensor may maintain the IPR during the contract
— The Licensor may be obliged to act against an infringer of the IPR</td></tr>
<tr><td></td><td>•
•</td><td>**Confidentiality**
Considering the need for following
— Recruitment freeze
— Prohibition of competition
— Separate NDA</td></tr>
<tr><td></td><td>•</td><td>**Specifications of licence**
— Exclusive or non-exclusive licence
— Related services
— Purpose of use (home, public, companies)
— Environment (company, territory or industry specific)
— Device specifications
— Period specifications (perpetual, made for the time being, limited time)</td></tr>
</table>

(*Continued*)

Table 10.9. (*Continued*)

	— Exact definitions (assignment, transfer, lease, sell, partially/completely)
	• **Rights and responsibilities of licensor**
	— Proprietary rights — Licensors right to improvements and upgrades of licensee
	• **Rights and limitations to use the software**
	— Rights to mature modifications — Combining to other product — Manufacturing, production, and restrictions — Sub-licensing (terms and limitations) — Obligation to exploit — Commercial rights (full/limited) — Copying
	• **Licence fees (single-premium, threshold price, royalty, redemption**
Safeguarding	• **Warranties** • The Licensor may be required to warrant that a licensed product or service conform to the order, the specifications in the agreement, and are delivered on time • **Liabilities and limitations**
	— Often a Licensor will undertake to repair or replace a defective product, but not be liable for any consequential loss the Licensee or its own customer may suffer — Liabilities for direct damages and consequential damages have to be stated — Terms of time when risk of loss or damage passes from Licensor to Licensee
	• **Transfer of contract** • **Other businesses** • *Force majeure*
Contingency management	• **Re-negotiations** • **Index clause** • **Transfer of contract** • **Mergers and acquisitions** • **Bankruptcy** • *Force majeure*
Dispute settlement	• **Choosing the best procedure for resolution of disagreements, management, of performance problems and infringements**
	— Private governance: negotiations — Third party governance: arbitration, mediator
	• **Liquidated damages** • **Applied law**

set by the owner of a product, service, or technology on how the licensee is legitimately able to use, combine, modify, and distribute the property of the licensor. In a licence agreement it is important to specify the quality and extent of these rights. This licence must clearly define the use of the rights that is permitted and the use which is forbidden, as well as the duration of the agreement.

Software licence agreement

A software licence agreement is an agreement which authorizes the licensee to the property of the licensor (see Table 10.10), and states the ways in

Table 10.10. Check-list for software licence agreements.

Notices	• Software licence agreement
	• Rules of open source community
	• Other related and previous agreements
	  — NDA
	  — Service agreement
	  — Collaboration agreement
	• Sales terms
	• Standard contracts, general conditions

Regulation	• No special enactment • General contractual principles • CISG (Sale of goods) • Commercial law • Copyright law, all software is copyright protected, except Public Domain • Patent law • Tax law • Product liability • Employment law • Competition law
SOFTWARE LICENCE AGREEMENT Frame	1. Parties 2. Object of agreement and introduction 3. Definitions of special terms used in contract 4. Licence management 5. Possible co-development 6. Possible related services 7. Contract management 8. IP management 9. Safeguarding 10. Contingency management

(Continued)

Table 10.10. (*Continued*)

	11. Dispute settlement
	12. Term of contract
	13. Terms of termination of contract
	14. Applied law

Co-ordination

- **Contract management**
  - — Organization (who, how, when, etc.)
  - — Timetable
  - — Price
  - — Terms of payment
  - — Reporting
  - — Sales terms
  - — Follow-up

- **Possible related co-development (see collaboration agreement)**
  - — Shared goal
  - — Roles and responsibilities of licensor and licensee
  - — Mechanisms for developing and follow-up the collaboration
  - — Rights to use other subcontractors

- **Possible related services**

Licence management

- **Definition of IP**
- **If the software is protected by a patent, registered design etc., then usually:**
  - — The Licensor either warrants that it owns the IP which does not infringe on third party rights
  - — The Licensor may maintain the IPR during the contract
  - — The Licensor may be obliged to act against an infringer of the IP

- **Confidentiality**
- **Considering the need for following**
  - — Recruitment freeze
  - — Prohibition of competition
  - — Separate NDA

- **Specifications of licence**
  - — Licensor is an application developer or service provider
  - — Exclusive or non-exclusive licence
  - — Related services
  - — Purpose of use (home, public, companies)
  - — Environment (company, territory, or industry specific)
  - — Device specifications
  - — Period specifications (perpetual, made for the time being, limited time)
  - — Exact definitions (assignment, transfer, lease, sell, partially/ completely)

(*Continued*)

Table 10.10.   (*Continued*)

	• **Rights and responsibilities of Licensor**
	— Proprietary rights
	— Licensors right to improvements and upgrades of licensee
	• **Rights and limitations to use the software**
	— Rights to mature modifications
	— Combining to other product
	— Manufacturing, production and restrictions
	— Sub-licensing (terms and limitations)
	— Obligation to exploit
	— Commercial rights (full/limited)
	— Copying
	— Number of users
	— Concurrent users
	— Publication
	— Escrow-terms
	— Shareware
	• **Licence fees (single-premium, threshold price, royalty, redemption)**
Safeguarding	• **Warranties**
	— The Licensor may be required to warrant that licensed software conform to specifications in the agreement, conform to the order and is delivered in time to meet the requirements of the order
	• **Liabilities and limitations**
	— Often a Licensor will undertake to repair or replace defective software, but not be liable for any consequential loss the Licensee or its own customer may suffer
	— Liabilities for direct damages and consequential damages have to be stated
	— Time when risk of loss or damage passes from Licensor to Licensee
	• **Transfer of contract**
	• **Other businesses**
	• *Force majeure*
Contingency management	• **Re-negotiations**
	• **Index clause**
	• **Transfer of contract**
	• **Mergers and acquisitions**
	• **Bankruptcy**
	• *Force majeure*
Dispute settlement	• **Choosing the best procedure for resolution of disagreements, management of performance problems and infringements**
	— Bilateral governance: negotiations
	— Third party governance: arbitration, mediator
	• **Liquidated damages**
	• **Applied law**

which the licensee can use, combine, modify, and distribute the property of the licensor. In a software licence agreement it is important to specify the quality and extent of these rights. There has to be a clear definition of permitted use of the rights and actions that are forbidden. The duration of the right of use also has to be agreed in a software licence agreement.

Consultant agreement

Consultant agreement is an agreement of consultancy between a consultant and a client. A formal, well-planned contract is important in this collaboration. The emphasis is on defining the role and assignment of the consultant. According to the patent law, the owner of the invention is the inventor; therefore this situation may have to be changed by contracts. Therefore IP management is considered to be important in this kind of collaboration. Rights for background and results have to be clarified clearly from the beginning. The check-list for the consultant agreement is presented in Table 10.11.

Table 10.11. Check-list for consultant agreement.

Notices	•	Consultant agreement
	•	Standard contracts, general conditions
	•	NDA
	•	Other related and previous agreements
Regulation	•	No special enactment
	•	General contractual principles
	•	Copyright law
	•	Patent law
	•	Employment law
	•	Competition law
CONSULTANT	1.	Parties
AGREEMENT	2.	Object of agreement and introduction
Frame	3.	Definitions of special terms used in contract
	4.	Roles and responsibilities
	5.	Contract management
	6.	IP management
	7.	Safeguarding
	8.	Contingency management
	9.	Dispute settlement
	10.	Term of contract
	11.	Terms of termination of contract
	12.	Applied law

(Continued)

Table 10.11.   (*Continued*)

Co-ordination	• **Roles and responsibilities**
	— The Consultant agrees to sell the work to Client who agrees to buy it
	— Clear definition of the "work"
	— Status of Consultant, whose representative he is, rights of decisions
	— Rights and responsibilities of Client
	— Consultants right to use subcontractors
	• **Contract management**
	— Project organization, who, how, when, etc.
	— Timetable
	— Compensation
	— Terms of payment
	— Reporting
	— Follow-up
IP management	• **Definition of IP**
	• **Specifications of background and results**
	— Rights to the background; background is often listed and defined in agreement or appendices for preventing disagreements considering the ownership
	— Rights to the results: according to patent law the owner of invention is the inventor, therefore this situation have to be changed by agreement in case the Client wants to own the IP
	— Copyright of Consultant
	• **If the work includes background or IP from Consultant, then usually:**
	— The Consultant who warrants it owns the IP which does not infringe any third party's rights
	— The Consultant may be obliged to act against an infringer of the IP
	• **Confidentiality**
	— Intention to patent has to be considered in a confidentiality agreement
	• **Considering the need for the following:**
	— Recruitment freeze
	— Prohibition of competition
	— Separate NDA
Safeguarding	• **Warranties**
	— The Consultant may be required to warrant that the quality and results of consulting conform to the specifications of the agreement

(*Continued*)

Table 10.11. (*Continued*)

	● Liabilities and limitations
	— If the Consultant intends to limit its liability, this should be stated
	— Often Consultant may not be liable for any consequential loss the Client or its customer may suffer
	— Terms of liabilities for direct damages and Consequential damages
	— Terms of time when risk of loss or damage passes from Consultant to Client
	● Transfer of contract
	● Other businesses
	● *Force majeure*
Contingency management	**● Re-negotiations**
	● Index clause
	● Transfer of contract
	● Bankruptcy
	● *Force majeure*
Dispute settlement	**● Choosing the best procedure for resolution of disagreements, management of performance problems and infringements**
	— Bilateral governance: negotiations
	— Third party governance: arbitration, mediator
	● Liquidated damages
	● Applied law

Table 10.12. Check-list for supply agreement.

Notices	●	Supply agreement
	●	Sales terms
	●	Standard contracts, general conditions
	●	NDA
	●	Other related and previous agreements
Regulation	●	No special enactment
	●	General contractual principles
	●	CISG
	●	Commercial law
	●	Copyright law
	●	Patent law
	●	Tax law
	●	Employment law
	●	Competition law

(*Continued*)

Table 10.12. (*Continued*)

SUPPLY AGREEMENT Frame	1. Parties 2. Object of agreement and introduction 3. Definitions of special terms used in contract 4. Shared goal 5. Roles and responsibilities 6. Contract management 7. IP management 8. Safeguarding 9. Contingency management 10. Dispute settlement 11. Terms of termination of contract 12. Term of contract 13. Applied law
Co-ordination	• **Roles and responsibilities** — The Supplier agrees to sell the products or services to the Buyer who agrees to buy them — The rules of the supply; obligation to supply a fixed quantity, only to order, only in case of sufficient inventory, etc. — The rules of exclusivity or non-exclusivity if the supplier has other buyers for the same product or service — Suppliers right to use subcontractors • **Contract management** — Project organization; who, how, when, etc. — Timetable — Price — Terms of payment — Reporting — Costs — Taxation — Sales terms — Approval of the results and invoicing
IP management	• **Definition of IP** • **If the delivery is property of Supplier and is protected by a patent, registered design etc., then usually:** — The Supplier warrants it owns the IP which does not infringe a third party's rights — The Supplier must maintain the IPR during the contract — The Supplier may be obliged to act against an infringer of the IP

(*Continued*)

Table 10.12. (*Continued*)

- **If the ownership of delivery transfers to Buyer, terms of this has to be agreed:**
  — At what point the ownership and the liability transfers to Buyer
  — In what extent the rights transfer
  — Rights to use may transfer but not the ownership
  — **If there is licence, see Licence agreement**

- **Confidentiality**
- **Are the following applied?**
  — Recruitment freeze
  — Prohibition of competition
  — Separate NDA

Safeguarding
- **Warranties**
  — The Supplier may be required to warrant that products supplied conform to specifications in the agreement, conform to the order and are delivered on time

- **Liabilities and limitations**
  — If the Supplier intends to limit its liability for a defective supply, this should be stated
  — Often a Supplier will undertake to repair or replace defective delivery, but not be liable for any consequential loss the Buyer or Buyers own customer may suffer
  — Chaining the liabilities, who is liable in supply chain
  — Terms of liabilities for direct damages and consequential damages
  — Terms of the time when risk of loss or damage to the delivery passes from Supplier to Buyer
  — Terms of time when the ownership of the delivery passes from the Supplier to Buyer

- **Transfer of contract**
- **Other businesses**
- *Force majeure*

Contingency management
- **Re-negotiations, hardship**
- **Index clause**
- **Transfer of contract**
- **Bankruptcy**
- *Force majeure*

Dispute settlement
- **Choosing the best procedure for resolution of disagreements, management of performance problems and infringements**
  — Bilateral governance: negotiations
  — Third party governance: arbitration, mediator

- **Liquidated damages**
- **Applied law**

Supply agreement

Supply agreement is an agreement between a supplier and a buyer for the supply and purchase of products, services, technology, or software. In general, this is a stand-alone agreement, but it may be a part of a broader arrangement, such as a franchise agreement or part of a system integrator's contract network, where the system integrator could have a net of different supply agreements to manage. The most crucial issues in supply agreements are agreements on terms of delivery and on liability. It is also crucial to define who owns the related IP and that it does not infringe a third party's rights. A check-list for the supply agreement is in Table 10.12.

Concluding Remarks

In the book *Bazaar of Opportunities for New Business Development — Bridging Networked Innovation, Intellectual Property and Business* (Paasi *et al.*, 2012) we wrote that in order to be successful in open innovation, an actor must understand its own role and interests as well as those of the opponents, know the value of the offering in question, be creative and skilful in negotiating and agreeing, and understand the business model in question and what opportunities and limitations that will create. This book, *Workbook for Opening Innovation — Bridging Networked Business, Intellectual Property and Contracting*, gives guidance and tools for all of this. The workbook gives practical tools and guides for business managers, R&D managers, innovation managers, IP managers, project managers, legal counsels, contract designers, etc., to successfully implement open and networked innovation in their business; in the development of new business as well as in the renewal of existing business. Both forms of business development are important, and could benefit from the involvement of external actors in one way or another. The tools in this workbook have been presented without any detailed discussion of the reasons why they are important. Such arguments have been given in the book *Bazaar of Opportunities for New Business Development*.

The tools presented in this workbook are generic. Some customization is always required when a firm would like to successfully implement them in their own business. We also remind the reader that many tools and guides related to networked business, IP strategy, and contracting are not independent but strongly interconnected. It reflects the fact that in a successful business, these three perspectives (networked business, IP, and contracting) are strongly interlinked. In many organizations, however, that is not the case. Instead, business management, networking, R&D, and legal perspectives more or less "lead their own life". It is a major message of the book that these perspectives should be incorporated in order for the organization to navigate successfully in the landscapes of open and networked innovation and business.

Although this workbook includes tools supporting the opening of innovation, we underline that any tool should not be taken as an end in itself. The power of tools is in that they force decision makers and other key people involved in the opening of innovation and new business development to systematically consider issues of high importance. It is the experience of the authors that, without support for systematic considerations, some important viewpoints may not be taken into account when planning or executing open and networked innovation activities. Some of the tools presented in this workbook are such that you have to follow the guidance of the workbook only a few times. After that they will become routine, and you will complete systematic considerations more or less automatically. On the other hand, there are tools, like the check-lists for contracts, which you have to come back to from time to time, unless you are preparing such contracts frequently.

The final note of the book concerns the opening of innovation which should not be taken as an end in itself. Opening of innovation to external actors is beneficial in many situations, but there is often an alternative option, doing the R&D fully in-house with your own commercialization. Therefore, one of the key questions for a firm throughout the innovation process is, whether it is beneficial to do the work alone, or is it actually the case that external knowledge is useful or even required? In the book *Bazaar of Opportunities for New Business Development — Bridging Networked Innovation, Intellectual Property and Business* we discussed scenarios and criteria for when the opening of innovation is most beneficial for a firm and concluded that opening of innovation is most valuable in a turbulent, dynamic environment; in an environment under fast, and perhaps disruptive, technological changes and/or environment where the needs of customers are changing. These findings were not simply generated by the authors but the results of others studies of open innovation (Savitskaya, 2011; Schweitzer *et al.*, 2011). Stable technological and market environments, on the other hand, are more in favour of in-house R&D, unless a firm is willing to break the stability in markets and create some turbulence on the markets through technological or business innovations. And causing market turbulence through an innovation is seldom a bad idea. So why not implement opening of innovation in your new business development?

Glossary

In this part of the book we define the central terms used in the workbook. We would like to note that for some terms there is no single and common definition available in the literature although there is consensus on a few similar definitions. There may also be small differences in the exact meaning of terms between disciplines. Definitions used in this glossary apply to the use of the terms in the chapters of this workbook.

Agreement of non-competition

Agreement that limits the employee's right to work for a competitor or to engage in such operations as an independent entrepreneur. This applies after the employment relationship has ended.

Applicable law

The law applied to the contract. It may be specified in the contract, but if not, the rules of private international law of the country determine the applicable law.

Arbitration

Legal procedure for the resolution of disputes outside the courts, where the disputed case is settled by one or more arbitrators. The arbitrator's decision is binding for both sides. Arbitration can be mandatory or voluntary, and can be binding or non-binding. These issues have to be set in an arbitration clause in contract. Mandatory means that the parties voluntarily agree to hold all disputes to arbitration.

Association

Association, in general, refers to a group of individuals who voluntarily enter into an agreement to accomplish a shared goal. Industrial associations are formed by specialists of a certain knowledge area, who have an interest in sharing and creating knowledge, and developing the area and their own knowledge base. As an employee, the specialist may need his employer's permission in order to participate in the activities of an industrial association. It is important that the employee understands the strategic importance of knowledge management (e.g. sharing and protection of confidential knowledge) in such participation.

Background (knowledge)

In the context of contracts, background can mean all IP and knowledge which the party had before agreeing the contract, which shall remain the exclusive and sole proprietary of the owner despite of the collaboration. The other parties may get the right to use the other party's background during the contract. A contract may define all background information, ownership and rights related to it which needs to be protected and managed.

Benchmarking forum

Benchmarking forums consist of actors who enter into an agreement to share knowledge about certain area in order to learn from each other. The participants of benchmarking forums are firms, when individuals are typically the actors in associations.

Business model

A business model describes how an organization creates, delivers, and captures value. It defines the offering (what), customers (to whom), value chain (how), and earning logic (how much).

Business strategy

Business strategy describes the sources of competitive advantage for a company and the methods in which they are implemented and sustained.

Business user community

Business user community refers to a group of actors who voluntarily enter into an agreement to share their knowledge of certain problem related to their work. Business user community is not provided by a certain firm (*see* **User/client community**).

CISG (Convention on Contracts for the International Sale of Goods)

Convention that establishes uniform rules applied to sales contract for the legal rights and obligations of the seller and the buyer. If not agreed otherwise, CISG rules apply to the sales contracts between the countries that have ratified the convention, when the business locations of parties are in different contracting states or when the connecting factor rules of private international law leads to apply the legislation of this state.

Closed business model

A business model of an organization is said to be closed when the actual innovation and new business development actions take place inside the organization with no involvement of external actors in innovation.

Co-creation network

A form of networked innovation where the intention is to create new knowledge together with (an)other actor(s) or share tacit knowledge between the actors. Interaction and shared processes between the actors are required and partner's commitment to co-creation is ensured by shared goals.

Co-development agreement

An agreement between two or more parties, that sets forth the nature of their co-development. The intention of co-development typically is research and development (R&D) or goals aimed at new innovations. The crucial issues in such an agreement may include terms concerning IP management, particularly the intent of the parties to background and results, co-ordination and a shared goal. *See also* **Collaboration agreement**.

Collaboration agreement

An agreement between two or more parties, that sets forth the nature of their collaboration. A consortium may consist of a wide variety of actors. Depending on the company's alignment and role, the emphasis of contractual elements and terms are different. Agreeing on collaboration can be also a part of another agreement, for example a part of a retail or software licence agreement. In collaboration agreements it is crucial to define obligations of parties, sharing of IP, rights to background information and outcome, sharing of profits and costs. Headlines and procedural rules have to be agreed clearly, but specifications can be completed later. *See also* **Co-development agreement**.

Confidentiality agreement

See **Non-disclosure agreement**.

Confidentiality protection

Confidentiality protection means the protection of trade secrets or other confidential information. The International Organization for Standardization (ISO) defines it as "ensuring that information is accessible only to those authorized to have access". It is considered as an informal method for knowledge protection in this workbook as it may be applied to knowledge that may not qualify as intellectual property in the sense of law. *See also* **Non-disclosure agreement**.

Consultant agreement

An agreement between two or more parties, including a consultant and a principal, that sets forth the nature of their collaboration. Consultant agreements are not regulated by any special enactment. In such agreements the emphasis is on defining the role and assignment of consultant and IP management. Rights for background and results have to be clarified clearly in the agreement.

Contingency management

Capability of adjusting to changing circumstances in business and contractual environments. Contingencies should be managed through all dimensions of contracting capabilities (content, process and network). In contract contents, contingency management may mean, for example, re-negotiation and index clauses.

Contract management

Contract management is how contract documents, contract processes, and network aspects of contracts are managed in a company. Planning, designing, drafting, signing, implementing, co-ordinating, following-up, managing contingencies, addressing related problems, monitoring contractual relationships, as well as terminating the contract and regulating the post-contractual time, are included in the field of contract management.

Contract process

Contract process means how contracting is arranged and organized in a firm or in a network. It covers the life cycle of contracting. Contract process starts from planning, goes through designing, drafting, and negotiating to signing. The process continues with implementation, co-ordination, follow-up, contingency management until a controlled termination of the contract.

Contracting

Contracting is making and implementing contracts in practice, understanding of contracts not only as documents but as means of control and co-ordination as well as reaching of business goals. It includes all the activities concerning contract contents, contract process, and network aspects of contracts. *See* **Contract management**.

Contracting capabilities

Corporate contracting capabilities are capabilities of a firm to use individual capabilities of an organization and harness them to design, maintain, and manage contracts and commitments. Contracting capabilities can be divided into three dimensions: contents capability, process capability, and network capabilities.

Contractual protection methods

Set of methods for knowledge protection that are based on written contracts between two parties and governed by contract law. Contractual protection methods include, e.g. confidentiality agreements, prohibition of competition clauses, and proprietary and access rights clauses in agreements.

Copyright

Set of exclusive rights granted to the author or creator of the original work, including the right to produce, copy, distribute, and adapt the work. The protection is available for both published and unpublished works. Copyright does not protect ideas, only their expression or fixation.

Cross-licensing

A contract in which two parties license to each other parts of their own IP portfolio with agreed terms.

Default rules

Default rules are rules in the laws that fill the gaps in incomplete contracts. Therefore default rules can be modified by agreement of the parties. Contract law can be divided into two kinds of rules: default rules and mandatory rules. *See* **Mandatory rules**.

Design/Industrial design/Registered design

A form of intellectual property rights that protects the appearance of a product in the course of trade. National laws often require product designs to be registered. Design rights and trademarks overlap to a certain extent because the appearance of a product may also be registered as trademark.

Employee invention

Invention made by an employee working for an employer. The invention has to be related to the work of the employee under the employer. According to legislation on employee inventions, the employer is allowed to claim the right for the invention, usually in exchange for fair compensation.

Evolving contract

A contract which is intentionally incomplete to be completed or adjusted during its life span.

Exclusive licence

An exclusive licence in intellectual property law is a licence by which the licensor transfers all rights other than the title of the property to the licensee. National laws often require an exclusive licence be registered. An "exclusive" licence used in business may often be a non-exclusive licence with additional exclusivity clauses such as geographical exclusivity or field of use exclusivity. *See also* **Non-exclusive licence**.

Explicit knowledge

Knowledge is said to be explicit when it has been or can be articulated, codified, and stored in certain media, for example as text, formulas, software code, or blueprints.

Flexible contract

A contract which is understood to be a means to flexible co-ordination and not understood as an unchangeable document. Changes can be made based on a contractual clause or renegotiations. One example of a flexible contract is an evolving contract. *See* **Evolving contract**.

Force majeure (Vis major)

Contractual clause which exempts contracting parties from fulfilling their contractual obligations for events and causes that could not be anticipated or are beyond their control. Events of *force majeure* are events beyond the control of either party which occur after the time of signing of agreement and which were not reasonably foreseeable at the time of signing of the agreement and whose effects are not capable of being overcome without unreasonable expense and/or loss of time to the other party. Events of *force majeure* often include, e.g. war, strike, and acts of government, natural disasters, fire, and explosions. Standard contracts often include a *force majeure* clause.

Formal protection methods

Intellectual property protection that is defined as property interests in law and governed by IP legislation. Formal protection methods include patents, trademarks, utility models, rights to trade names, and copyrights.

Franchising

Franchising is a contract-based business between two actors, where a franchisor gives a franchisee rights to practice business by using another firm's business model or brand name.

Freedom of action

The effect of the patent or other IP on the ability to conduct business in strategically important markets without the risk (or with reduced risk) of being sued for infringement.

General conditions (standard contract)

Part of contract or the entire contract document in which the rights, responsibilities, and obligations are modelled or itemized for the contracting parties.

Implementation of work

Phase of work when the contractual responsibilities are performed. Implementation may start from the signing of a contract, but it is recommendable to define the start in the contract. Contracts may be designed proactively so that flexibility and opportunities to modify and develop the agreement (evolving contract) can be adapted in the implementation phase. Implementation of contract requires continuous inter-firm collaboration as sharing of roles and tasks, communication, and follow-up.

Influence in business environment

Company's ability to affect the future markets for technology or competences and steer (technological) development in a favourable direction with the IP.

Informal protection methods

Set of methods for knowledge protection that is based on companies' internal processes or policies rather than legislation. Informal protection methods attempt to prevent the loss of key knowledge or restrict undesirable access to sensitive information either inside the firm or in external relations.

Innovation

A new idea that can be commercialized and is significantly better than an earlier solution. The innovation can relate to products, services, technologies, business and organizational models, operational processes, or operational methods.

Innovation inter-mediator, Innovation mediator, Innovation broker

Terms used in business management literature for an actor that helps firms to transgress their own boundaries and access external knowledge or utilize external innovators. The roles of innovation inter-mediators can be divided into: Innovation consultants, Innovation traders, Innovation incubators, and Innovation mediators.

Innovation mediator platform

Innovation platform provided by an innovation mediator (*see* **Innovation mediator**) in order to link together innovators and needs of firms and facilitate the innovation process between them. Innovation (inter-)mediators control their platform and form the rules for the interaction and rewarding.

Intellectual property (IP)

In general, the term "intellectual property" may include any rights resulting from intellectual activity in the industrial, scientific, literary, or artistic field. Often the term "intellectual property" is used as a synonym of "intellectual property rights" (IPR). In this workbook the term "intellectual property" is used broadly to include not only IP rights that are granted and protected by the laws, but also the knowledge and other intangible resources whose use may be controlled by contracts, policies, organization, and process routines and norms, both physically and technically.

Intellectual property agreement

Agreement between or among collaborating parties concerning the rights and responsibilities of each party pertaining to the intellectual property relevant to the collaboration. Agreement may be limited to the outcome of the collaboration which may be jointly developed or may include IP brought in to the collaboration or developed independently by each party. *See* **Background (knowledge)**.

Intellectual property rights (IPR)

Intellectual property rights are exclusive rights granted by the national laws over the inventions, creations, and signs, which provide for the right holders the rights to prohibit others from exploiting and using the inventions, creation, and signs. Intellectual property rights include patent right, utility model, trademark, design right, and copyright. *See also* **Intellectual property**.

IP evaluation

Company's practices related to estimating potential benefits and other effects that a single IP asset would yield to the company, when utilized in company's business in some defined way. The analysed potential benefits are often derived from a company's IP strategy, and the IP evaluation itself is used in decision making regarding that IP.

IP monitoring

Practices and activities for observing activities (publication, prosecution, litigation, expiration) surrounding IP related to relevant technologies outside the company, charting the IP of the most important participants in company's market and industry areas, and checking against possible conflicts with own IP.

IP portfolio

A set or collection of IP assets of a company, protected by formal, contractual, or informal methods.

IP programme

A part of a company's IP strategy describing the process-related issues, responsibilities, and policies of IP management. Includes, e.g. procedures for managing, reviewing, and monitoring IP, company confidentiality policies, and employee education practices regarding IP.

IP prosecution

The process of seeking a formal IP protection (usually a patent or other registration-based protection) in compliance of procedural aspects of national intellectual property laws leading to a rejection of a grant of a right from authorities such as patent and trademark offices.

IP strategy

A coherent awareness of a firm as to what knowledge is important for the company and how the IP should be protected, managed or shared in order to support the business model and business strategy of the company. IP strategy focuses both on knowledge that can be controlled with formal intellectual property laws, and also knowledge and other intangible resources whose use may be controlled by contracts, policies, organization, and process routines and norms, both physically and technically.

Joint venture

A contractual business undertaken by two or more parties (firms or other legal entities). Joint ventures can be distinct business units or collaborations between businesses. Joint venture agreement between two or more parties sets forth the nature of their collaboration, specifies their mutual responsibilities, rights, and shared goal. Such an agreement may define the intent and the shared goal of their collaboration and the limitations to it.

Letter of intent (LOI)

Interim agreement expressing intentions to conclude a contract in the future. Letter of intent differs from preliminary agreement in its binding. This document does not oblige further agreements, as a preliminary agreement containing the main points of a proposed deal does. Also called memorandum of understanding (MOU) or pre-contract.

Liability

Obligation incurred by a contract party usually due to its defaults, negligence, or other problems in the performance of contractual obligations.

Liability does not require negligence by a party. Contract parties may decide and define the extent of the liability they are willing to accept and ensure in a contract document.

Licensing, Licence agreement

An agreement by the right holder (licensor) permits another party (licensee) to use the underlying intellectual property. "Use" may include various economic actions such as making, using or selling, reproducing, and offering for sale, and is defined in national laws. Licence agreement may be permanent or temporary, exclusive or non-exclusive. Often, a licensor may receive a royalty or other remuneration. *See also* **Open source community**.

Mandatory rules

Parts of the law that have to be complied with. Mandatory rules are obligatory legislation. Mandatory rules will be enforced even if attempts to modify or override them are made. *See also* **Default rules**.

Memorandum of understanding (MOU)

See **Letter of intent (LOI)**.

Networked innovation

Networked innovation or business is related to the opening of business development and innovation processes over the company borders. Networked innovation (business) is defined as having the following characteristics: (i) there is a specific shared vision (goal) about collaboration, (ii) the process is seldom open for everyone, although multiple actors are involved in the innovation, (iii) the collaboration covers both the knowledge transfer and the co-creation activity between actors, (iv) there is a contract either written or otherwise formed between the involved actors, and (v) the co-ordination is based on both control-governance and self-organization. Innovation and business relationships are divided into co-creation and transaction networks according to the strategic role of knowledge.

Non-disclosure agreement (NDA)

An agreement that imposes duty of non-disclosure to the parties agreeing to it used for ensuring the confidentiality of ideas, business secrets, and other confidential material. NDAs are either one-way or mutual. In such an agreement, the scope of the confidential information should be defined, as well as the period during which information will be considered confidential. A NDA can be made in business transactions as well as in employment. During the employment relationship confidentiality is also protected by law, but extending the period of the confidentiality to time after the employment, contractual protection is necessary. Between business partners first confidentiality documents are usually set in the beginning of negotiations and can be considered to support the openness between actors from that stage. Confidentiality agreement is very common in companies.

Non-exclusive licence

Non-exclusive licence may be a licence with exclusivity limited to a specific scope or field, such as context, market, territory, or time. In its weakest form, a non-exclusive licence is a simple promise of the licensor not to sue the licensee for IP infringement. *See* **Exclusive licence**.

Open business model

A business model of an organization is said to be open when part of the innovation related to the value creation, value delivery, and value capturing of the organization is done by external actors, i.e. the organization applies open/networked innovation. *See also* **Business model** and **Open innovation**.

Open forum/platform

Open forum or platform for interaction and knowledge sharing. The most informal model of co-creation networks, where it is not possible to know all the participants.

Open innovation

Open innovation means that, in addition to their internal ideas and technologies, organizations use external ideas and technologies in their own business, and let their unused ideas and technologies be used by others. *See also* **Networked innovation**.

Open source community

Open source community is a user-based community of OSS developers and programmers, which is loosely regulated by the norms as well as the terms of OSS licences. The community consists of both individuals and companies, who share an interest in participating in the development of certain software, which is usually developed in a collaborative manner. Open source licence presents the rules on how this software can be utilized for commercial purposes. Although open source communities are based on peer-to-peer production between equal participants, there are different levels of participation and there are different roles of participation.

Open source software (OSS)

Open source software is software which is distributed with its source code. OSS is usually distributed with a particular software licence that permits licensees to change, modify, distribute, and commercialize the software in varying degrees. Open Source Initiative (OSI) exists to maintain the quality of OSS and approves the licence which fulfils the terms of Open Source Definition (OSD). When passing the acceptance procedure of OSI the licence may have the "open source" certification.

Patent

To exclude others from making, using, offering for sale, or selling an invention without permission. National laws define these rights but WTO-TRIPs (World Trade Organization trade-related aspects of intellectual property rights) agreement harmonizes the national laws and requires WTO member states to provide minimum standard of protection. The invention must meet the national standard of patentability such as novelty, non-obviousness/inventive step and utility/industrial applicability. Additionally, a patent applicant needs to follow the formal procedure of patent application (prosecution). In many countries the protection is granted for 20 years from the filing date.

Preliminary agreement

Preliminary agreement may be considered as a binding contract to agree on a final contract and its validity may be the same compared to further contracts. A preliminary agreement can be concluded when all the important issues related to the contract or collaboration are not clear in the beginning of collaboration. In co-creation networks, the preliminary agreement could be considered as the first step towards a binding collaboration.

Private ordering

Private ordering describes private parties' own attempts to regulate themselves as opposed to public ordering by governments, legislation, and courts.

Private ordering includes informal rules and code of conducts as well as such methods as contracts and disputes settlements outside the court systems. *See also* **Arbitration** and **Public ordering**.

Product differentiation

Price premium or increased sales resulting from unique product features (or unique features of the offering in general) attributable to the IP.

Public domain

In the context of IP law, public domain refers to works, ideas, and information, which are publicly available.

Public ordering

Regulation of behaviours by the public authority. Public ordering includes both mandatory and non-mandatory legislation, preliminary rulings, and other judicial decisions. It may be due to the regulation of the state or other public entity as well as court ordering. *See also* **Private ordering**.

Publishing

Publishing is the process of production and dissemination of information available for public view. Publishing as a method of knowledge protection prevents others from appropriating the knowledge, thus confirming the freedom of action for the firm. Publishing can also be used to prevent other companies from claiming patents in the same area.

Recruitment freeze

An agreement where the parties agree that they do not attempt to recruit each other's personnel without the consent of the other party. Recruitment freezes can be used only temporarily.

Secrecy

Form of informal method for knowledge protection which means that key knowledge is kept secret from outsiders either from some of the employees inside the company and/or from external co-operation partners such as customers and business partners. *See* **Confidentiality protection**.

Shared goal (vision)

Shared goal or vision represents a network's common understanding about the future benefits of networking, joint actions to reach these benefits and participants' roles, responsibilities, and rights. The shared goals (vision) are formed, at least partially, within a negotiation process by all the network companies.

Software licence agreement

Contract between the licensor and licensee for the right to use the software. The licence agreement may define the terms under which the copy can be used. It is a definition of the owner of a work or software of how is the licensee legitimate to use, modify, and spread the property of licensor. Such an agreement authorizes the licensee to the property under the incorporeal rights. It is important to define the quality and extent of the rights. Both permitted and forbidden use of the rights have to be defined clearly. The duration for the right of use has to be agreed. *See also* **License agreement**.

Standardization

Standardization is the process of developing technical specifications based on the consensus among all interested parties in a given industry. The process may be voluntary or mandatory. The main objective of standardization is typically to achieve interoperability among products of different companies.

Strategic alliance

Strategic alliance is a formal contractual relationship between two or more parties to pursue a shared goal. Strategic alliance considers joining of forces, capabilities or resources, for a specified or indefinite period. There are several types of strategic alliances: (i) equity alliance is an alliance in which two or more firms own different percentages of the company they have formed, (ii) non-equity alliance is an alliance in which two or more firms develop a contractual relationship, and (iii) joint venture in which two or more firms create a legally independent company.

Subcontracting

Action done by a prime contractor to hire a subcontractor to perform a specific task of the overall project or work. Subcontractors are under a subordinate contract to the prime contractor. The purpose of the subcontract may be for example supply of materials, services, labour, etc.

Sub-licensing

The grant by a licensee of certain licensed software or technology to license to a third party.

System integrator

A network actor capable of bringing together high-technology components, subsystems, software, skills, knowledge, engineers, managers, and technicians in order to produce a product or service in co-operation with other suppliers.

Tacit knowledge

Form of knowledge that is difficult to articulate in a way that is meaningful and complete. The fact that we know more than we can tell describes the tacit dimension of knowledge. Sharing of tacit knowledge requires extensive personal contact and interaction between the actors.

Technology strategy

Technology strategy describes which technological areas are important for the company and how the technological knowledge helps create competitive advantage for the company.

Trade secret

Information that is not generally known to the public, confers economic benefit, and is the subject of reasonable efforts to maintain its secrecy. A trade secret can be a formula, practice, process, design, instrument, pattern, or compilation of information which is not generally known or reasonably ascertainable, and by which a business can obtain an economic advantage over competitors or customers. Trade secrets are protected without registration and can be protected for an unlimited period of time. Trade secrets are protected by law and illegal disclosure of trade and commercial secrets is sanctioned in criminal law.

Trademark

A trademark right is a form of intellectual property protection granted to signs that are often visibly recognized including words, symbols, shapes, and images. Some countries protect sounds as well as smells as trademarks. Subject to national laws, following the procedure of registration, a registered trademark is protected against use of the identical or similar marks in the course of trade, in relation to registered goods or services. Some countries protected unregistered trademarks, where marks have been used as a trademark and have acquired source identification function.

Transaction network

A form of networked innovation where (existing) knowledge is acquired by a transaction. The direction of transaction may be from outside to inside, when a company is acquiring explicit knowledge (IP) from another actor, or from inside to outside, when company is selling, licensing, or donating own generated explicit knowledge (IP) to another actor. Typically, the relationships and the contracts in transaction network are bilateral.

User/client community

Community provided by a firm for the users (business-to-consumer) or clients (business-to-business) of its products or services. Participants can share their experiences, discuss and learn from each other, and often firms utilize the community to collect ideas for business development purposes.

Utility model

A utility model, also called "a small patent", is a form of intellectual property right that provides a lower cost right which is usually restricted to products rather than processes. It has a shorter term and weaker coverage than a patent and it is not examined for validity prior to grant. Utility models are practical when the invention is intended for a domestic protection only for a relatively short period of time.

References

AIPPI (International Association for the Protection of Intellectual Property). www.aippi.org (Accessed on 27 February 2012).

Bader, M.A. (2006). *Intellectual Property Management in R&D Collaborations: The Case of the Service Industry Sector*, Physica-Verlag, Heidelberg.

Bauwens, M. (2006). The Political Economy of Peer Production, *Post-Autistic Economics Review*, No. 37, pp. 33–44.

Blomqvist, K., Hurmelinna-Laukkanen, P., Nummela, N. and Saarenketo, S. (2008). The Role of Trust and Contracts in the Internationalization of Technology-intensive Born Globals, *Journal of Engineering and Technology Management*, Vol. 25, pp. 123–135.

Chesbrough, H. (2003). *Open Innovation: The New Imperative for Creating and Profiting from Technology*, Harvard Business School Press, Boston.

Chesbrough, H. (2006a). Open Innovation: A Paradigm for Understanding Industrial Innovation, in Chesbrough, H., Vanhaverberke, W. and West, J. (eds.), *Open Innovation: Researching a New Paradigm*, Oxford University Press, Oxford, pp. 1–12.

Chesbrough, H. (2006b). *Open Business Models: How to Thrive in the New Innovation Landscape*, Harvard Business School Press, Boston.

Chiaromonte, F. (2006). Open Innovation through Alliances and Partnership: Theory and Practice, *International Journal of Technology Management*, Vol. 33, pp. 111–114.

Dahlander, L. and Gann, D.M. (2010). How Open is Innovation? *Research Policy*, Vol. 39, pp. 699–709.

DeBresson, C. (1999). An Entrepreneur Cannot Innovate Alone; Networks of Enterprises are Required, DRUID Conference on Systems of Innovation, Aalborg, Denmark.

Dittrich, K. and Duysters, G. (2007). Networking as a Means to Strategy Change: The Case of Open Innovation in Mobile Telephone, *Journal of Product Innovation Management*, Vol. 24, pp. 510–521.

Eckhard, B. and Mellewigt, T. (2006). Contractual Functions and Contractual Dynamics in Inter-firm Relationships: What we Know and How to Proceed, University of Paderborn working paper no. 88. Available at SSRN, http://ssrn.com/abstract=899527 (Accessed on 29 March 2012).

Gassmann, O. and Enkel, E. (2004). Towards a Theory of Open Innovation: Three Core Process Archetypes, R&D Management Conference, Lisbon, Portugal.

Gollin, M. (2008). *Driving Innovation — Intellectual Property Strategies for a Dynamic World*, Cambridge University Press, Cambridge.

Haapio, H. and Haavisto, V. (2005). Sopimusosaaminen: Tulevaisuuden kilpailutekijä ja strateginen voimavara, *Yritystalous*, Vol. 2, pp. 7–15.

Henkel, J. (2006). Selective Revealing in Open Innovation Processes: The Case of Embedded Linux, *Research Policy*, Vol. 35, pp. 953–969.

Huizingh, E. (2011). Open Innovation: State of the Art and Future Perspectives, *Technovation*, Vol. 31, pp. 2–9.

Hytönen, H. and Jarimo, T. (2008). From Scenarios to Lattices: Flexibility in Portfolio Optimisation, International Federation of Operational Research Societies (IFORS) Conference, Sandton, South Africa.

IfM and IDM (2007) *Succeeding through Service Innovation: A Discussion Paper*, Cambridge University Press, Cambridge.

Laursen, K. and Salter, A. (2006). Open for Innovation: The Role of Openness in Explaining Innovation Performance among U.K. Manufacturing Firms, *Strategic Management Journal*, Vol. 27, pp. 131–150.

Lichtenthaler, U. and Lichtenthaler, E. (2009). A Capability-based Framework for Open Innovation: Complementing Absorptive Capacity, *Journal of Management Studies*, Vol. 46, pp. 1315–1338.

Lopez, H. and Vanhaverbeke, W. (2010). Connecting Open and Closed Innovation Markets: A Typology Intermediaries, DIME conference organizing for networked innovation, also available online at http://emma.polimi.it/emma/events/dimeconference/attachments/henry%20lopez-vega.pdf (Accessed on 29 February 2012).

Luoma, T., Paasi, J. and Valkokari, K. (2010). Intellectual Property in Inter-organisational Relationships, *International Journal of Innovation Management*, Vol. 14, pp. 399–414.

Maxwell, E. (2006). Open Standards, Open Source and Open Innovation. Harnessing the Benefits of Openness, *MIT Press*, Issue 3, pp. 119–176.

Möller, K., Rajala, A. and Svahn, S. (2005). Strategic Business Nets — Their Type and Management, *Journal of Business Research,* Vol. 58, pp. 1274–1284.

Mowery, D. (2009). Plus ca Change: Industrial R&D in the "Third Industrial Revolution", *Industrial and Corporate Change*, Vol. 18, pp. 1–50.

Nystén-Haarala, S. (ed.) (2008). *Corporate Contracting Capabilities*, Conference proceedings and other writings, Publication of Law of the University of Joensuu 21. Joensuu.

Nystén-Haarala, S., Lee, N. and Lehto, J. (2010). Flexibility in Contract Terms and Contracting Processes, *International Journal of Managing Projects in Business*, Vol. 3, pp. 462–478.

Open Source Initiative. www.opensource.org (Accessed on 29 February 2012).

Päällysaho, S., and Kuusisto, J. (2008). *Intellectual Property Protection in Service Sector,* available online at http://www.iccwbo.org/uploadedFiles/ICC/policy/intellectual_property/pages/IP%20protection%20in%20service%20sector.pdf (Accessed on 16 March 2012).

Paasi, J., Luoma, T. Valkokari, K. and Lee, N. (2010). Knowledge and Intellectual Property Management in Customer-supplier Relationships, *International Journal of Innovation Management*, Vol. 14, pp. 629–654.

Paasi, J., Valkokari, K., Erkkilä, J., Hakulinen, J., Kirveskoski, K. and Räisänen, V. (2011). Levels of Openness in Open Innovation, Proceedings of 2011 ISPIM Conference, Hamburg.

Paasi, J., Valkokari, K., Rantala, T., Nystén-Haarala, S., Lee, N. and Huhtilainen, L. (2012). *Bazaar of Opportunities for New Business Development — Bridging Networked Innovation, Intellectual Property and Business*, Series on Technology Management, Imperial College Press, London.

PRO INNO Europe (2007). *A Memorandum on Removing Barriers for a Better Use of IPR by SMEs*, A Report for the Directorate-General for Enterprise and Industry by an IPR Expert Group.

Savitskaya, I. (2011). *Environmental Influences on the Adoption of Open Innovation: Analysis of Structural, Institutional and Cultural Impacts*, Acta Universitatis Lappeenrantaesis 439, Lappeenranta University of Technology.

Schweitzer, F., Gassmann, O. and Gaubinger, K. (2011). Open Innovation and its Effectiveness to Embrace Turbulent Environments, *International Journal of Innovation Management*, Vol. 15, pp. 1191–1207.

Sterman, J.D. (2000). *Business Dynamics: Systems Thinking and Modeling for a Complex World*, McGraw-Hill, New York.

Swan, J. and Scarborough, H. (2005). The Politics of Networked Innovation, *Human Relations*, Vol. 58, pp. 913–943.

Teece, D.J. (1998). Capturing Value from Knowledge Assets: The New Economy, Markets for Know-how, and Intangible Assets, *California Management Review*, Vol. 40, pp. 55–79.

Välimäki, M. (2009). *Oikeudet tietokoneohjelmistoihin*, Talentum, Helsinki.

Valkokari, K., Paasi, J. and Rantala, T. (2012). Managing Knowledge within Networked Innovation, *Knowledge Management Research and Practice*, Vol. 10, pp. 27–40.

van de Vrande, V., de Jong, J., Vanhaverbeke, V. and Rochemont, M. (2009). Open Innovation in SMEs: Trends, Motives and Management Challenges, *Technovation*, Vol. 29, pp. 423–437.

Van Wijk, L. (2005). *There May Be Trouble Ahead — A Practical Guide to Effective Patent Asset Management*, Scarecrow Press, Lanham, Maryland.

West, J. and Gallagher, S. (2006). Challenges of Open Innovation: The Paradox of Firm Investment in Open-source Software, *R&D Management*, Vol. 36, pp. 319–331.

Williamson, O. (1985). *The Economic Institutions of Capitalism: Firms, Markets, Relational Contracting*, Free Press, London.

WIPO (World Intellectual Property Organization), http://www.wipo.int/about-ip/en/ (Accessed on 29 February 2012).

Wright, I. and Fergusson, C. (2009). Contracting Principles, IACCM, An Opportunity for Leadership — 09 Contracts Trends and Projections.

Index